MATT DUGGAN

DETECTIVE SERIES

EPISODES I–V

JONBLAIR

Edited by Kristen Corrects, Inc.
Cover art design by Shutterstock.com
Typesetting by Kingsman Editing Services

ISBN: 979-8-9895376-3-1 (paperback)
ISBN: 979-8-9895376-5-5 (e-book)

Fiction>Crime>Drama>Detective
Fiction>Crime>Drama>Gangster

First edition published 2024

CONTENTS

THE CASE OF THE MYSTERY PHONE CALL

———

EPISODE I

PROLOGUE

After his former partner is murdered, Private Investigator Matt Duggan sets out to find the killer. Join Matt and his capable assistant as they unravel a scheme involving a crooked cop on the mob payroll, their plan to move a load of cocaine worth millions, and a guarantee to kill anyone who gets in the way.

PART I

My name is Matt Duggan. I'm a licensed private investigator, twice divorced, without children or any other pesky dependents. I retired after twenty-three years with the Metropolitan Police Department, working my way up the ranks as a road patrol officer before transferring to the Homicide Unit as a rookie gumshoe. I've been on my own for the last eleven years and, at age fifty-five, busier than a one-eyed cat watching nine rat holes. For the first several years I worked informally for several insurance companies, conducting arson, wrongful death, and other phony and fraudulent claim investigations, my harried schedule made more organized and tolerable due to the efforts of my assistant, Delia Perez, a former paralegal, widow, gorgeous, bilingual, competent, and thorough at her job. I keep her as up to date as I can on every case I'm working, to include my whereabouts at all times—and talk about intuitive, she's helped on more than one occasion solve an investigation simply by throwing a couple of "what ifs" in my direction.

Delia was on the phone as I walked into my agency on what started as a pleasant, but late Monday morning.

"Matt, it's for you."

I stopped and stood next to her desk. "Who is it?" I asked.

"Don't know," she replied with her usual, beautiful smile. "Whoever it is said it's urgent and they need to speak with you right away."

"Transfer it to my office," I replied. Delia nodded, pushing the transfer button on her dialer, and my phone immediately rang as I walked in and closed the door behind me.

"This is Matt Duggan," I answered. "Who am I speaking to?"

"Never mind that right now," came the frantic reply from an unknown male, sounding middle-aged. "I don't have time to tell you anything over the phone other than I need to retain your services. Someone we both know told me to call you. Can you meet with me this evening at the airport?"

I paused, fixated on the "someone told me to call you" part of his reply. "Where at the airport?" I asked, picking up on the caller's urgency.

"There's an abandoned hangar next to Moody Aviation—be there at eight."

"What's this about?" I asked in a futile attempt to glean more information, but the caller ended the brief conversation with the distinctive *click* of a telephone receiver being dropped on its cradle.

I slowly placed the handset back on its ringer. *Someone we both know?* I thought to myself, staring out the window behind my desk. I had no clue, but the fact the caller indicated it was someone familiar to both of us interested me further. It could involve someone I knew who was in trouble, someone who might be mixed up in whatever it was the caller was involved in. I glanced at my watch—eight hours until meeting time.

I grabbed my coat and walked out of my office, briefing

Delia on my conversation with the unknown caller. She was concerned about me meeting this prospective client alone, particularly with his refusal to identify himself or provide any information as to exactly why he wanted to meet.

"Not to worry, I'm on my way to pay a courtesy call to Detective McPherson with Homicide at Metro PD," I informed Delia. It wasn't unusual to meet with detectives at Metro PD periodically, or for them to drop by my agency to exchange information about open cases each side was working. "I'll ask him to tag along with me this evening," I assured her.

"Isn't he the guy who replaced you when you retired?" Delia asked, relieved I wouldn't be meeting this guy solo.

"That's him," I said, smiling. "I've known Seth McPherson a long time—good friend of mine, and a good cop. He saved my ass on more than one occasion." I paused, remembering for a moment before continuing, "If I'm not back later, I'll see you tomorrow." It was my oft-repeated "goodbye for the remainder of the day" quote. I threw my sports jacket over my shoulder and walked out the door.

I relaxed, or tried to, for an hour while I had lunch at my usual greasy spoon cafe, making small talk with the owner and his wife, just long enough that it didn't interfere with the enjoyment of my meal. Still, I couldn't shake the thought about the "it's someone we both know" comment.

After lunch, I spent the remainder of the day traveling to and talking with various clients and other sources regarding pending cases. The more serious the case, the greater priority it was given, homicide always being at the top of the list. A reminder app on my iPhone brought to mind my involvement in the Police Family Survivors' Association, created to serve the families of law enforcement officers killed, disabled, or paralyzed in the line of duty. Another officer and I volunteered our time to mentor surviving adolescents and teenagers. As a former law enforcement officer, I witnessed firsthand the devastating impact that death or traumatic injury caused a law enforcement officer's family. On a deeper level, perhaps it was my way of filling a void brought on by never having children of my own. Nevertheless, I enjoyed being a part of it.

Right before five p.m. I pulled into the parking lot at Metro PD, exited my vehicle, and made my way up to Homicide. Everyone at MPD knew me; access was never a problem.

When I reached his office, he wasn't there. "Where's McPherson?" I asked, looking around.

"Good question," replied his longtime partner, Sergeant Leah Mulholland. "He left about noon, didn't say a thing about where he was going or when he'd be back, which is not unusual for McPherson. Did he know you were coming?"

"No, he didn't, it was just a drop-by."

"If he returns or calls, I'll let him know you were here," Mulholland quipped indifferently, shuffling through a pile of jumbled-up paperwork as she stood hunched over his desk, never glancing in my direction.

I thought her activity was somewhat peculiar, the fact she was rifling through papers on her partner's desk. *Something doesn't seem quite kosher*, I thought, storing that observation in the back of my mind.

"Appreciate it," I responded disingenuously. I had no interest in engaging in small talk with McPherson's partner. I always believed her to be an insufferable putz. My flippant tone didn't faze her in the slightest as she continued to shuffle through the disorganized pile of papers. I could never understand how or why McPherson put up with her.

I made it home by six p.m., grabbed a quick meal, checked my mail and messages, straightened and organized a few things around the house. I would be attending this initial meeting alone. I pulled my .38-caliber Charter Arms short-barrel revolver out of its holster and opened the cylinder; it was fully loaded. I snapped the cylinder back into place and returned the revolver back to its holster, which was secured to my belt just above and to the right of my back pocket, my sports coat conveniently concealing the weapon.

I left my home around seven fifteen and made it to the airport hangar just before eight. I parked and exited my vehicle, noticing the small hangar was built with hangar bay doors on the side facing the airport runways, and a regular entry/office-type door on the opposite side facing the main highway. The building appeared abandoned by its overall disheveled appearance, accentuated by weeds growing in its asphalt parking lot and overgrowth of landscaping.

I walked to the entry door, noticing it was closed, but not fully shut. I took another look around, then grabbed the doorknob and slowly pulled the door open. It was dim but not dark inside, as it was the middle of summer and light still filtered through the many windows. I left the front door open to allow in what little light of the day remained.

It was eerily silent—something didn't seem quite right.

I pulled my snub-nose .38 out of its holster and cautiously walked through the front door. There was a small office immediately to my right with its door open. I continued quietly until I reached the office door, took a quick look inside, and saw nothing. I turned and again walked slowly, staying close to the outside office wall. As I reached the front end of the office, I looked discreetly around the darkened corner—and lying face down was the body of a male, fully clothed in a suit.

I placed my revolver back into its holster, reached down and turned the corpse over, staring in total disbelief. "Holy shit, it's McPherson!"

PART II

I was still reeling from the shock of discovering McPherson as I leaned against the first MPD vehicle to arrive on scene. I provided only basic information to the road patrol officer, preferring to wait until the chief detective made his appearance, which, as it turned out, would not be long. The neglected hangar bay parking lot began to light up like an unplanned Christmas event as one emergency and police vehicle after another, sirens blaring and lights flashing, dutifully followed the other onto the worn-out asphalt. The emergency lights seemed to bounce off the aluminum hangar in a blended but disorganized manner, reminding me of the old-style tinsel Christmas tree as it joyfully changed color with each turn of the rotating wheel. This situation was anything but joyful.

A four-door sedan came barreling into the lot, heading straight toward the marked vehicle I was leaning against, its flashing lights acting like a beacon. For a moment I wasn't sure the sedan had any intention of stopping, when finally, the driver slammed on the brakes. Forward momentum continued to propel the skidding vehicle to a halt only a few feet away from me. All four doors flew open like they were spring-loaded, the vehicle emptying in record fashion as the first occupant, followed by three others, sped in my direction.

I knew immediately who the point man was, followed by McPherson's partner, Sergeant Leah Mulholland.

"Okay, Duggan, start talking, what happened?" Chief Detective Louis Sullivan angrily asked, as if my presence had somehow precipitated the murder of his best detective.

I filled the chief detective in on the details regarding all I had seen and heard, beginning with the phone call earlier in the day, my visit to MPD later in the afternoon, and finally, the discovery of Detective McPherson's body only an hour prior. Other than turning the body over, I told the chief nothing else had been tampered with. We walked into the hangar as I recounted and pointed out step-by-step the ground I had previously covered, right up to the discovery of McPherson's body. Crime scene technicians gathered informally in a huddle before slowly fanning out to begin the task of evidence gathering, assisted by the two detectives accompanying the chief. It wasn't lost on me that Sergeant Mulholland remained eerily silent, seemingly preoccupied with the activity of the technicians as they now took full charge of this part of the investigation.

"How do you feel about this, Duggan, what do you think?" the chief detective turned and asked. The anger in his voice was not as noticeable now, after I filled in the blanks, the information corroborating everything I had told him.

"Like I've been double punched in the gut, that's how I feel," I replied, feeling sick to my stomach and suppressing my own anger as I grabbed a pack of Rolaids out of my jacket. As I removed four out of the roll and chewed slowly, glancing at the technicians, I silently replayed the entire day's events in my head.

"Any idea about the identity of the caller?" Chief Sullivan asked.

"Didn't recognize his voice," I answered truthfully, "but I'll have Delia obtain the phone number tomorrow," I assured the chief.

"All right, we'll call it a night for you, Duggan. Go home, get some rest, be at my office at ten in the morning. We'll finish up here and notify McPherson's family. I appreciate your help," the chief added as he gave a comforting pat on my shoulder.

I glumly nodded as I faced the hangar's front door, the inside now lit up like a Hollywood movie stage as technicians illuminated the entire area like a football stadium, the investigation in full swing. Before I took a step, I turned again in the direction of Chief Sullivan.

"Hey Chief, what is it with Mulholland?"

"What do you mean?" he replied, a perplexed expression on his face.

"I mean she hasn't said two words the entire time we've been here. She was McPherson's partner, for Christ's sake. I find that pretty damn odd, don't you?"

The chief detective glanced in the direction of Sergeant Mulholland, who was now walking around solo, nowhere near the crime scene technicians, almost as if she was conducting her own separate investigation.

"I'll talk with her," the chief responded, shaking his head slightly as a curious grin etched itself across his face. "See you at ten a.m.," he repeated, his attention now focused on the quizzical behavior of Sergeant Mulholland.

I nodded. "I'll be there."

PART III

My assistant picked up on the second ring as I called the office the following morning en route to Homicide at MPD.

"Morning Delia, I'm on my way to MPD to—"

"Matt, I need you here, now," she replied abruptly, a sense of urgency clearly perceptible in her voice.

I was befuddled for a moment. "What's going on, Delia?" I asked, the tone of my voice confirming I was aware she was in trouble.

A male's voice now responded to my question. "You need to do what the little lady just told you." I immediately recognized it to be the same unidentified caller I spoke with the previous morning. "Oh, and don't call the cops," he added. "I'd hate to do anything to her pretty face because you did something stupid."

"I'm on my way," I said, making a U-turn to race to the agency.

Ten minutes later I pulled into my parking space, hurriedly walking toward the office before cautiously opening the front door. Delia was sitting at her desk, an apprehensive look on her face as we made eye contact. The unidentified man stood behind her, his right hand holding what appeared to be a .38-caliber revolver, resting the gun on her shoulder.

"All right, I'm here," I announced calmly, trying not to rattle the visitor. "Now . . . what's this all about?"

Before he could answer, Delia blinked twice followed by a loud *BOOM*. The exterior window shutters throughout the office closed in unison, slamming down on the metal windowsills like a flashbang grenade.

Startled, the visitor dropped his gun. Delia bounced out of her chair and pushed the man in my direction. I grabbed the lapels of his suit jacket, yanking him away from Delia and simultaneously hitting him with a glancing blow to the head. He fell forward against a row of metal shelves before grabbing a three-hole punch, turning and wildly swinging the metal punch in my direction. I kicked the punch out of his hand, followed by a left hook and straight right to the jaw, connecting solidly with both, slamming him backward and against the wall before he slid butt first to the floor. Delia tossed a set of handcuffs she kept in her drawer as I positioned our unconscious visitor face down and cuffed him.

"Great timing," I complimented Delia, grinning.

"Great idea installing those spring-loaded shutters with the release button under my desk," she responded. "Our wink code worked perfectly."

"Absolutely did," I replied, pleased at how well our distraction ploy worked. "Dial 911. Let's get a squad car down here so they can book this yo-yo. I'll move our guest to the sofa and see if I can get him to talk before he goes on his joy ride to the big house."

"He's out cold, Matt. Can you check his jacket for a cell phone and ID before you move him?" Delia asked. She tapped 911 on her desk phone.

"Thanks for reminding me. I told the chief detective

I'd get this guy's phone number; his cell phone could be a treasure trove. Ah, yes, here we go," I said, reaching into the inside pocket of his suit jacket and removing a smartphone, then his wallet.

On the phone, Delia provided information in response to the canned 911 prompt, "State your emergency." She hung up. "MPD is on the way," she said.

I briefed her on the previous evening's sequence of events, and she made clear her disapproval of my decision to meet our guest without backup.

"Travis Moore," I voiced out loud after removing a driver's license from a disheveled billfold, carefully reviewing the information on the laminated document. He had two hundred dollars and a few credit cards, several phone numbers written on folded pieces of paper stuffed in the wallet, but nothing else of significance, and no photos. I dragged him by the shoulders and lifted him up onto the sofa as he started to come around. I swapped the driver's license, wallet, and cell phone for a damp washcloth Delia handed me while she photocopied the license. I patted his red and swollen face with the damp cloth. He jerked his head away as he regained consciousness.

"I'll run his license and complete the usual background checks on . . . Mr. Moore," Delia said as she carefully reviewed his driving permit.

He finally appeared alert enough for questioning.

"Okay, Travis, I'll ask you again, what's this all about?"

Before he had a chance to respond, the sound of tires squealing resonated throughout the office.

Delia turned her attention to the front door. "Sounds like the cavalry has arrived." She was correct: Seconds later, the door flew open and three uniformed officers raced inside, guns drawn, followed by Chief Detective Sullivan.

I was surprised by the appearance of the chief. "What are you doing here?"

"You were late for your appointment, then I got wind of the 911 call," he replied. "I thought they might be related. What did this joker tell you?"

"Nothing. I just started to question him when you and your officers came barreling through the door."

"Well, he's under arrest and coming with us," Chief Sullivan dictated, using his authority to override my preference to question him before he was booked. "By the way, your new appointment is at four p.m. today, be there." His officers snatched Travis off the sofa, escorting him to one of several cruisers, lights still flashing as a crowd gathered. The chief stooped down to pick up the revolver Travis had dropped earlier, then added, "And you can pick up your cuffs when you get there." A wry smile appeared on his face.

"Yeah, thanks, Chief," I replied in a cynical tone.

"Forgetting something, Duggan?" the chief detective asked, walking slowly around the office before stopping and staring at me knowingly.

"Like what?" I replied, aware of what he was referring to.

"Wallet, cell phone." He paused, then added, "ID if you removed it from his wallet."

I reluctantly nodded to Delia, who handed the items to the chief.

"Oh, I forgot to ask—are you and Delia okay? Either of you hurt?"

Delia and I looked at one another, half disgusted with the manner in which the chief detective appeared to be soft-pedaling the entire episode, beginning with my assistant being held hostage.

"No Chief, we're just ducky."

PART IV

Chief Detective Sullivan was sitting behind his desk viewing his open laptop when I walked into his office at exactly four p.m. I was particularly eager for a briefing regarding any additional information discovered about Travis Moore.

"Reporting as ordered, Chief," I announced in a flippant tone, still irritated about the earlier felonious event at my office and the subsequent downplay by MPD.

"Have a seat, Duggan," he said, pointing as he continued staring at his computer screen.

"What's going on with Mr. Moore? What can you tell me about this yahoo?" I knew Delia was running the usual background checks on the suspect as the chief and I began our meeting. It was my intention to compare information gleaned by MPD against whatever Delia was able to dig up.

"We released him an hour ago; he's not being charged with anything," the chief detective responded, closing his laptop and turning in my direction.

"You did *what*?" I shouted, staring incredulously at the department's head detective, my rhetorical question another way of asking, *What are you, a total idiot?*

"We found nothing on the guy; we had to let him go," the chief retorted angrily, pissed off I had indirectly labeled him a moron.

"He walked into my office and held my assistant at gunpoint," I reminded Sullivan. "What do you call it, a neighborly visit by the welcome wagon?"

"Any witnesses other than you and Delia?" the chief asked, an angry expression still on his face.

"You know there wasn't," I reminded him again. "What about the gun?"

"He has a permit to carry a concealed weapon, and he has no criminal record," the chief replied.

"He had no permit in his wallet or clothing, and you found his gun on the floor of my office," I responded sarcastically.

"Maybe he dropped it," the chief replied.

"So, I simply beat the hell out of this guy for no reason other than he just walked into my office?"

"You're lucky I don't arrest you for aggravated battery, Duggan. Fortunately for you, Mr. Moore very generously decided not to press any charges. You're free to go."

"I'm free to go?" I parroted. "That son-of-a-bitch contacted me yesterday, refused to identify himself, and asked me to meet him at an abandoned airport hangar. He doesn't show up, and instead I discover McPherson's body. I told you everything I know when you and your team arrived on the scene. The next day Travis Moore decides to pay an unannounced visit to my office and takes Delia hostage. Why, as a way of thanking her for her pleasant personality? No one except Travis Moore knows the reason for any of this, and you don't see a connection? What kind of half-assed investigation are you conducting? Does McPherson's family know how you're handling this? And by the way, what's with Sergeant Mulholland and all that weird shit she's been doing?"

Chief Sullivan rose from his chair. "Get out of my office, Duggan," he snarled, articulating every word.

We glowered at each other before I finally stood. "McPherson was my former detective partner and good friend," I began, staring directly at the chief. "I have every intention of speaking with his wife and family. If they want me to continue this investigation, that's exactly what I intend to do. You're obviously not getting anywhere."

"Better watch your step, Duggan. You're walking on thin ice."

"What exactly does that mean, Chief? Is that a warning or a threat?"

"It means I can have your license suspended, maybe even revoked—you're not a cop anymore. I don't want you talking to McPherson's family until I'm finished with *my* investigation," he ordered.

"Try and stop me," I responded curtly, grabbing my jacket and exiting his office. I knew Sullivan and his "boys" would be watching me. It dawned on me the chief and his colleagues might be hiding something, and I was determined to find it.

I was on my way to McPherson's home when I received a call from Delia.

"Yes, Delia, what's up?"

"Matt, you're not going to believe it," she exclaimed. "I just discovered Moore's driver's license is a phony. The DMV has no record of a 'Travis Moore' based on the license information. It's not him, Matt. What did you find out at MPD?"

"Nothing—they let him go, claimed he had no criminal background."

"And the office brawl, holding me at gunpoint?"

"No witnesses—our biased word against his," I answered.

"What now?" Delia asked.

"I have a contact in the FBI. I'll see if I can coax him into pulling prints off the three-hole punch he used to try to put a hole in *my* head. Otherwise, I'm on my way to Seth's home. Keep the doors locked. I'll be there as soon as I finish speaking with the McPherson family."

"Be careful, Matt."

I stopped at a convenience station to refuel. While I stood behind the pump filling my vehicle, I glanced at what was rumored to be a popular restaurant next door. Checking out the parking lot, I couldn't believe my eyes. Exiting a Hyundai Sonata, Sergeant Leah Mulholland and the now-bogus "Travis Moore" began walking toward the restaurant's front door, talking all the way to the entrance. They were oblivious to my presence less than a hundred feet away. I fought the urge to confront them, as well as contact the chief detective, but opted to photograph the vehicle and license plate instead.

I left the gas station and drove to McPherson's home. There were two marked MPD vehicles in the front, both parked next to the curb. I continued down the street, turning onto a main thoroughfare before pulling into the parking lot of a laundromat. I grabbed my iPhone.

"FBI Regional Office, can I help you?" a pleasant voice asked.

"Agent Frank Morelli, extension 2301," I replied.

PART V

"His name is Jason Edward Smyth," Agent Morelli informed me, returning to his desk with a thin manilla folder, several documents partially visible outside the bottom of the file. I was seated on the opposite side of my agent friend's desk as we continued our conversation. He pulled out his chair, sat, then opened a drawer, swapping the file for a pair of reading glasses.

"We were able to retrieve and match his prints from the hole punch you provided," Morelli said, entering the last of several keystrokes on his desktop keyboard before pushing the enter button. "He has the usual lengthy record, from a teenager starting with nickel-and-dime stuff all the way to mob affiliation. He's been connected with several crime families for the last twenty years or so, never rising above the level of an associate, non-made member. Rumor has it he has collateral duties as an 'enforcer,' used as compliance muscle or for approved whacks," he continued, reading off the monitor before swiveling it in my direction.

"Yeah, I see that," I remarked, perusing the computer screen closely, the suspect's photo appearing in the upper left corner. "What's his status currently?"

Agent Morelli moved and clicked the mouse, the next page appearing with the same suspect photo. Stamped in red letters, the word PAROLED appeared diagonally across the entire page. Moving closer to the monitor, I noticed a parole date that extended back a little over two months ago. Further review of the computer file confirmed Jason Smyth was released on parole from Blackwater Correctional Center after serving eight years for labor racketeering, extortion, and arson, although he was considered a suspect in several other cold cases, including murder. At the time of his incarceration, he was associated with the Pozzallo Crime Family, with operatives in the greater metropolitan area, particularly in drug trafficking, extortion, loan sharking, theft of public funds, and labor racketeering.

"Is he currently under investigation or surveillance?" I asked.

"He is now," Morelli replied, rising from his chair. "We've got a paroled mobster with a phony driver's license somehow connected with a dead cop. The phantom phone call, your discovery of the murder, the incident the following day at your agency, and Smyth's unwarranted release tells me what *you* already know—it all appears connected. And as for Chief Detective Sullivan and Sergeant Mulholland, we'll add them to the investigation as well, free of charge."

"I take it MPD never informed you of McPherson's murder?"

"We were officially notified by the state's DLE— another red flag. That's the paper file you saw me throw in the desk drawer earlier. Has the McPherson family asked for your help on behalf of Seth?"

"I haven't had a chance to speak with his widow or adult children. It's entirely possible they believe the MPD is conducting an appropriate investigation. I told you about the marked vehicles outside the home—not unusual when one of their own has been killed in the line of duty. It's also possible their presence is to detect or deter my involvement. I didn't want to call Mrs. McPherson if the chief detective has her landline bugged. I don't know who has Seth's cell phone, but I can have Delia locate his wife's cell phone number."

"I could check the McPherson landline to confirm a tap, but it might alert MPD to our involvement," Morelli informed me. "For now, let's keep them believing you're the only other outside party investigating Seth's murder."

I nodded in agreement.

Agent Morelli opened his desk drawer again. He pulled out the manila file and handed it to me. "I've added a copy of the bureau's two pages you viewed earlier. Take a look at it and commit to memory whatever you believe is important. And just so we're on the same page, you didn't see this, or get it from me. Capisce?"

"Understood," I replied, my eyes capturing the information on the documents like a scanner.

I returned the file to Morelli and drove back to my agency.

It was later in the evening when I arrived. I unlocked the door and walked past Delia's desk and into my office, the dimmed banker's lamp on the opposite side of her computer monitor acting as a nightlight, revealing the general layout of the otherwise darkened room. I opened my office door and walked to my desk, stooping down slightly as I reached for a small flask of hooch I kept stashed in one of the drawers. I needed it. I poured a couple of "mud in your eye" gulps into one of several stained coffee mugs scattered sporadically on top of my desk. That was the last thing I remembered.

* * *

"Looks like he's coming around," a familiar voice echoed in the background. I instinctively moved my hand to the back of my head. I couldn't determine which was bigger, the knot on my skull or the migraine-size throbbing I felt. I winced, rolling until I finally managed to sit up, leaning against a concrete wall in a room I recognized as the same office outside of which I discovered the lifeless body of Seth McPherson. Visual acuity slowly returned, my focus sharpening until the distinct outline of Sergeant Mulholland and Jason Smyth, a.k.a. "Travis Moore" was crystal clear.

"How does it feel, hotshot?" Smyth asked, rendering a wry smile. He was holding my gun, obviously happy he now had the upper hand.

"I'll let you know after you're sentenced to life plus twenty-five," I retorted sarcastically. "You and your cohorts," I added.

Smyth walked angrily in my direction, probably to belt me a few times. Mulholland quickly grabbed his arm. "Forget it," she said. "We have bigger fish to fry right now. The plane will be here soon. Once we've unloaded the shipment, we can reload it with Mannix here and toss his gumshoe ass out over the desert somewhere. No one will ever find him."

Smyth grinned like a Cheshire cat. Mulholland's plan of disposal assuaged his anger. "Can't think of a better sendoff."

"Here, take some of these zip ties and bind our friend good and tight," she directed, extending her hand toward Smyth with the ties. "There's some duct tape in the desk drawer. Tape his mouth and blindfold him with your pocket square, then come out here and help me open the hangar doors. The plane should arrive with the five bales in about fifteen minutes. They'll contact me on my cell phone as soon as they land and begin taxiing toward the hangar."

"No problem," Smyth grunted, holding the ties in his left hand.

Mulholland turned and walked across the empty hangar bay, her steps fading as she neared the large sliding hangar doors. I could see she was wearing a bulletproof vest underneath navy blue coveralls, her 9mm Glock holstered and attached to a wide black utility belt.

"Okay, Duggan, face down on the floor, hands behind your back," Smyth bellowed, motioning with my gun still in his hand. When I began to comply with his order, he stuffed the revolver in his waistband. He then stood over me.

In an instant I rolled on my back, drew my right leg to my chest and kicked like a mule, nailing him squarely in the family jewels. He instantly dropped the ties and gun, reflexively grabbed his crotch, and fell to the floor with a soft thud. A low, guttural moan followed, confirmed by an agonized expression on his distorted face.

"How does it feel, hotshot?" I asked, mockingly returning his question. I flipped Smyth over and zip-tied his hands and ankles. I grabbed the duct tape out of the drawer and taped his mouth, then dragged him behind the desk and zip-tied him again to a corner leg. I removed my cell phone from his jacket, then picked up my revolver and walked cautiously to the partially closed office door.

It was dark throughout the hangar, the only illumination coming from just one of four fluorescent tubes secured to the office ceiling. Outside, I could hear Mulholland fumbling with the hangar doors. They were installed with a motorized opening mechanism, but the motors had apparently been removed, requiring they be opened manually using a chain and cable system. She continued to grope with the doors as I quietly walked toward her and the noise. She had placed her small service belt flashlight on the adjoining door handle, pointing it toward the doors. She heard my approaching footsteps, turning around and acknowledging my silhouette.

"About time you got here," Mulholland said, believing it was Smyth. "Give me a hand with these doors. The plane will be here soon; they'll be spooked if they taxi up to the hangar and the doors are still closed."

"Having a problem?" I asked.

Mulholland stopped fiddling with the doors, exhaling an exasperated sigh as she recognized my flippant tone.

"Don't even flinch," I growled.

Walking up behind Mulholland, I unsnapped and lifted the semi-auto Glock out of its holster, then depressed the magazine release button. I kicked it hard to the left after it hit the floor. I dropped the Glock and kicked it to the right, where it slid a good distance on the smooth concrete. I grabbed and scrunched a handful of shirt collar behind her neck and pushed the crooked cop back in the direction of the office, my revolver in my other hand. I directed her to a chair.

"Sit, and don't get up," I told her.

Smyth was on the floor in a fetal position, still moaning through the duct tape over his mouth. She rendered her partner in crime a disdainful and unsympathetic gaze, probably thinking he was an incompetent dumbass. I pulled my cell phone out of my pocket.

"Hold on, Duggan. Maybe we can work something out," Mulholland implored, realizing she would either spend the remainder of her life behind bars or have it terminated sooner by a mob family who didn't want her making turncoat deals with state or federal prosecutors. She was obviously throwing out some bait, wondering if perhaps I might bite. She didn't have anything to lose by trying, so I decided to play along.

"I heard you mention five bales. Continue," I said.

"Five bales of high-grade cocaine. Five million dollars to you if you let me go, leave, just walk away," she replied. "That's over thirty percent of its street value. A deal of a lifetime if you're smart enough to say yes."

"You'll have to do better than that. What about McPherson? Why was he killed?" I asked.

"He found out about tonight's drop. How, I don't know, so I lured him to the hangar and had Smyth whack him before he discovered my involvement."

"So that's why you were nosing around his desk the day I dropped by. You were looking for anything that McPherson had lying around that might connect you with tonight's drop."

"I knew you'd jump headfirst into it as soon as you were aware of his murder," she continued, "so I had Smyth call under the pretense of a client who needed your help. The plan was to whack McPherson, then you, then dispose of you both. The problem is my dumbass partner became impatient and went to a bar and grill after he whacked McPherson rather than waiting to take care of you. Instead, he got drunk and picked up some floozy, so we sent him to your office the next day to finish the job, but he screwed that up too."

"Who's we?"

"Chief Detective Sullivan," she answered.

"Yeah, I thought so," I replied, my anger reaching a boiling point. I decided to let state and federal authorities question her and arrest the chief detective regarding their involvement with the Pozzallo Crime Family. My current priority was to get Morelli and his agent colleagues here as quickly as possible, seize the plane and shipment, and arrest everyone involved.

"So, what do you think? Remember, we're talking five million dollars," she pressed.

I paused, trying to contain my fury. "You want to know what I think, Mulholland? I think I'd rather dive naked onto a pile of rabid porcupines than ever consider anything you have to offer. You murdered my partner, my friend, a husband and a father. Seth was a dedicated, decent cop and a good man. You are one cold, uncaring, murdering bitch, and a disgrace to law enforcement. You, Smyth, and the rest of your drug-dealing, murdering partner-in-crime mobster friends are going to prison for the remainder of your shitty lives. That's what I think."

Mulholland sat there, bewildered, like a deer in the headlights. She placed her hands on her face, bending her upper torso slowly forward as she began to cry—or at least that's what she wanted me to believe. She extended her hand toward the floor, removing a hidden .38-caliber backup revolver attached to her ankle. As she brought herself and the weapon upward, I raised my own gun and fired one shot, striking her squarely in the chest, slamming her backward and onto the floor. Her gun flew across the room, behind an old credenza cabinet.

She was flat on her back and unconscious, saved by her bulletproof vest, exchanging a toe tag for a dinner plate-size dark blue and purple contusion.

"I'm actually glad you were wearing that vest, Mulholland," I said out loud as I stood over her. "Seeing you go to prison for the reminder of your sorry life is the greater poetic justice."

She was starting to come around, moaning. Even with a bulletproof vest, a direct hit in the chest at point-blank range with a .38-caliber round is like being hit with a sledge-hammer. Her chest was going to hurt like someone dropped a cinderblock on it from two stories.

I zip-tied her hands and ankles and once more to the opposite corner desk leg. I grabbed my cell phone again just in time to hear the sound of an aircraft approaching the hangar. With the hangar bay doors still closed and Mulholland not picking up her phone, I guessed they'd wait no longer than a minute or so before turning the aircraft around. If I was wrong and they forced entry, I was a dead man walking for sure.

I ran across the hangar to a small observation window on one of the doors. *At least I could go down fighting*, I told myself. Hunkering down, my gun in one hand, cell phone in the other, I was a second away from pushing Morelli's contact cell number. It was then my eyes caught sight of a caravan of DEA and FBI tactical assault vehicles roaring around both sides of the hangar, lights flashing on every truck in an overwhelming show of force. They surrounded the aircraft, SWAT officers pouring out of the mobile pill boxes like hornets attacking an unwelcome intruder. At the same time, I could hear the sound of a ramming bar being used to force open the main entry business door, the same door I originally entered the day I discovered McPherson's body. I heard Agent Morelli's voice as the door burst open.

"Duggan, it's Morelli. Can you hear me?" he shouted, SWAT officers running en masse in front of him as they fanned out in every direction.

I holstered my revolver as a precaution. "Right here," I shouted, instinctively raising both arms. It was still dark inside the hangar, and I had no intention of being mistaken for one of the bad guys. "I'm walking in your direction."

"Everyone, it's Duggan, hold your fire," Morelli shouted, apparently recognizing my voice.

Morelli could finally see enough of me as I approached. He lowered and holstered his Sig Sauer P226 semi auto pistol, relief on his face. "You're certainly a sight for sore eyes," he said, smiling.

"Yeah, and you're beautiful too," I replied, reciprocating with my own smile, happy this miserable ordeal was finally over.

Morelli stopped two officers hurrying by him. "Let's get some lights on in here."

"We're on it," they answered.

"I brought someone who's even happier to see you than I am, Duggan," Morelli said as he turned around and motioned with his arm.

Delia was walking with a SWAT officer in our direction, a smile of relief so evident it could have lit up the entire room without the help of any lights.

"This lady probably saved your life, Duggan," Morelli began. "Delia called when she couldn't reach you at home or your cell phone. She told me she was calling to let you know she had a dentist appointment first thing in the morning and would be running a little late. She said she's always able to reach you after hours, either at home or on your cell phone, and that you never fail to get back to her within ten minutes. When you didn't return her call, she called me. I told her to meet me at your office. When we arrived, she immediately noticed your desk was slightly askew."

I turned and looked at Delia with a mixture of curiosity and bewilderment. "What was it you noticed?" I asked, my interest piqued.

"You left that flask on your desk, and the drawer you keep it in was open," she answered. "One of your coffee cups was tipped over, and your chair pushed off to the side. I know you, Matt—that's just not like you. You're too neat and tidy about little things like that. I knew something was wrong."

"I asked Delia to go with her gut about what she thought happened, or where you might be," Agent Morelli continued, "and she didn't hesitate to answer in three words: the hangar bay. She's one of a kind, Duggan. I'd hang on to her."

"Oh, I fully intend to," I replied, smiling as I put my arm around my intuitive assistant, pulling her close to me.

Officers opened the hangar bay doors and towed the aircraft inside with its load of high-grade stash. The aircraft's pilot and crew were handcuffed and led to waiting vehicles for transport to jail, along with Smyth and Mulholland. Morelli informed Delia and me that Chief Detective Sullivan was in the process of being arrested at his home as we spoke.

"Oh, if you don't mind, Frank, Delia and I would like to drop by the McPherson home tomorrow morning. We want to be the first to explain everything that's happened. The odds are probably one hundred percent they've been kept in the dark and bamboozled by Mulholland and Sullivan."

"I'm okay with that. McPherson's wife and family knew you and Seth were close. Let her know we'll be in contact as well, along with the DEA. The DLE will be conducting an extensive investigation regarding the Metropolitan Police Department. We'll need to know if there were any others involved."

Delia slipped her hand around my arm, tugging gently.

"How about an early breakfast, Matt, with plenty of coffee?" she suggested, still smiling.

"Hmm," I said as I raised my eyebrows. "As a matter of fact, I know of a very popular restaurant."

THE END

THE CASE OF THE MENACING NOTES

EPISODE II

PROLOGUE

A former client turns to Private Investigator Matt Duggan after receiving a series of threatening notes. Having come perilously close to losing his license years earlier after taking on this same client, Matt is wary of accepting her case a second time, until he's knocked unconscious by an unknown assailant while attempting to retrieve the notes in her apartment. Join Matt and his assistant Delia Perez as his investigation uncovers a crooked law firm, their army of thug enforcers, and a scheme to market millions of dollars of illegal opioids to an unsuspecting public.

PART I

Delia knocked and opened my office door simultaneously. "Sorry to interrupt, Matt—you have a visitor." A revealing smile on her face all but confirmed our walk-in and I were already acquainted. In this business, becoming re-acquainted isn't necessarily a good thing, and as events progressed, that would soon become apparent.

"Who is it?" I asked, shifting my attention from my computer monitor and glancing upward at my assistant.

"She wouldn't say," Delia answered, "but finally did blurt out, '*Matt and I know each other.*'"

I took a deep breath. "Tell her I'll be right there," I said, exhaling my reply. It was my usual practice to greet appointments or walk-ins, introduce myself after Delia's initial greeting, then engage in a polite amount of superfluous small talk. It was my way of making potential clients feel comfortable before inviting them into my office to discuss how I might be of help. Appears I'd be able to skip the "meet and greet" part this time around.

"Matt?" a female voice uttered as I exited my office.

I turned and locked eyes with an attractive middle-aged woman, my memory finally matching a face to a name. "Rebecca? Rebecca Blakely?" I said, a dubious smile working its way across my face. We embraced momentarily before I took a step back, my arms fully extended, my hands gently resting on her shoulders. "Rebecca, I can't believe it. How are you?" My arm's-length grip allowed me to thoroughly scan her face. First impressions told me she hadn't appeared to age a day since our last encounter more than ten years earlier.

"Matt, it's wonderful to see you again," she responded. "I was so afraid you wouldn't remember me, or at the very least without some reminiscent coaxing," she continued, laughing.

"Rebecca, it's—"

"Please, Matt. It's Becky, remember?"

I paused, then smiled. "As I recall, it was Becca, remember?" I playfully parroted.

"Yes, I remember," she replied, still smiling.

I placed my hand behind her elbow and guided her into my office, directing her to a small couch. I grabbed a chair in front of my desk and positioned it several feet away from the sofa, then sat. Time for "rubbing elbows" was over. I suspected from the moment I recognized her she didn't drop by on a whim to indulge in memorable past events; for all the wonders of modern technology, there was never a substitute for gut instinct. I motioned for Delia to come into my office. It was time to find out why Ms. Blakely was here.

"Lovely office," she said as she looked around, continuing her reticent façade.

"So, Becca, what brings you here?" I finally asked, the tone of my voice confirming the time for exchanging pleasantries was over. The smile on her face disappeared, quickly replaced by a foreboding expression.

"I need your help, Matt," she said, her tone now serious, her facial expression almost desperate. She stood and wandered around the office, as if the Sword of Damocles hovered over her.

I had a strong sense of déjà vu, recalling how my representation more than ten years earlier nearly cost me my license. "Tell me about it," I said, somewhat disingenuously. I was hesitant to become involved in another of Becca's serial tragedies. Truth be told, she was intelligent, beautiful, and ambitious, although at times misguided, with a penchant for trouble that followed her like a bad odor.

"I don't even know where to begin," she moaned, her words still trembling, confirming her flair for drama.

"It's usually best to start at the beginning," I suggested.

She continued to pace the office before finally blurting out, "I believe someone is out to hurt me—maybe even kill me."

"Kill you . . . for what?" I asked skeptically. My thoughts reverted to our investigator/client relationship of ten years earlier. It didn't take long at that time to figure out Becca had a proclivity for getting herself into one mess after another. Ten years later, and, if her hunch was correct, she'd now managed to piss *someone* off to the point her life might be in jeopardy. I shook my head slightly, letting out an exasperated sigh.

"Can you help me, Matt?" Her misty, piercing blue eyes pleaded for my approval.

I rose from the chair and walked back to my desk, then turned and sat on a corner. I placed a hand over my mouth, moving my index finger back and forth across my day-old mustache stubble, exchanging dubious glances with Delia. I was debating silently whether I wanted her as a client, particularly considering what she put me through the first time.

"Would it be too presumptuous to say you want me to

find out who this person is?" I asked, my question a half-baked yes to Becca's request for help.

Several weeks earlier, Rebecca Blakely was employed as a certified legal assistant with the prestigious law firm of Colby, Miller & Wright, a boutique firm located in the central business district. She had been with the firm just over three years, happily employed as a senior paralegal for one of the firm's founding partners—happily employed until recently, that is, when she inadvertently uncovered evidence they were helping several well-known pharmaceutical companies deliberately and aggressively market known addictive opioids. In addition, the firm was advising the companies on how to downplay the risks of addiction, that the drugs were safe, and to the contrary, underutilized. It had all the makings of a perfect storm.

A month later, and despite the fact she had not disclosed her discovery to anyone, she was called into her boss's office and summarily fired. No plausible explanation was given for her termination.

Another week went by before she received what she perceived as the first of several threatening notes. The first slipped under her apartment door, the second delivered through a slightly ajar window on the driver's side of her SUV while parked at a grocery store, and the third pushed through a louver on her locker at the local gym. Each note was more threatening in intensity and was composed of individualized clippings of letters or words glued onto dark-colored paper stock.

The common denominator appeared to be the perpetrator, who knew enough about Becca to deliver the notes where they made the most frightening impact. The last note implied she was talking to authorities, and that if she wanted to *remain healthy* she would cease and desist immediately.

She thought about contacting the police but believed it too risky. That's when she sought my help.

"I was really frightened, Matt, especially after the third note. If they really believed I was talking to the police, that last note convinced me my life was in danger. That's when I decided I to contact you."

"Do you have the notes with you?" I asked.

"I meant to bring them, but I was so agitated before I left my apartment earlier that I forgot. They're inside a computer desk drawer in my living room."

I grabbed my sports jacket on the coat valet. "Let's go to your place," I said, my response a confirmation I was officially on the case.

"Keep me posted," Delia reminded me as Becca and I left the office to drive to her apartment. I wanted to look at the "notes" she had described. It was sometimes possible to glean information from the evidence—in this case, the notes—depending on how they were worded or constructed. I also wanted to place them in a sealed baggie for fingerprint preservation. If the threats appeared credible, we would also need to bring the responsible police precinct into the investigation.

I pulled into a guest spot after a nearly thirty-minute drive. Becca's residence was a corner unit on the first floor. There was a backyard with two medium-size trees and another related apartment building separated by a small retention pond. It appeared to be well maintained.

"Very nice," I observed. "How long have you resided here?"

"I leased my unit shortly after I was hired by the law firm," she answered, pulling a key out of her purse and unlocking the front door.

We walked into Becca's apartment. It was of moderate

size, nicely furnished and decorated, a pleasant scent emanating from two electric fragrance warmers. There were framed photos in several locations of people I assumed were family members or friends. Becca placed her handbag and keys on the kitchen counter. Initially, nothing appeared out of the ordinary.

"Can I offer you something to drink?" she asked, opening the refrigerator door.

"A bottled water would be fine," I replied, completing my visual scan of her apartment. "But I would like to take a look at those notes," I added, a not-so-subtle reminder of why we were here.

Becca glanced at me and smiled. She slowly closed the refrigerator door, and without saying a word handed me the bottle of water then walked toward her computer desk. I followed her as she stood next to the chair, reached down, and opened a small drawer next to the keyboard tray.

"What the . . . ?" she called out, a puzzled look appearing on her face. Becca stuck her hand inside to rifle through the contents. She slammed the drawer shut and walked around the chair to the left side, opening the opposite drawer and brusquely scouring its contents.

"Well?" I asked in a skeptical tone.

The expression on her face answered my question. She looked at me with a mixture of befuddlement and shock. "They're not here!"

"What do you mean, they're not here?" I fired back, my mind locked in a moment of total recall, remembering from past experience Becca's inclination to exaggerate a current predicament, or create a new and potentially more dangerous problem.

"They were here, Matt!" she cried out a second time, becoming misty-eyed again.

Any sympathy and sentiment for the truth she had initially convinced me to feel was rapidly dwindling. "When you find what you're looking for, drop by the office," I said, disgusted I had wasted almost half a day on what I perceived as the proverbial wild goose chase. I turned and placed the unopened bottle of water on the counter, intending to leave her apartment. That's when she screamed . . .

And that was the last thing I remembered.

PART II

"How long have I been out?" I asked, sitting up and grabbing Becca's hand. She had been patting my face and forehead with a moist rag, kneeling next to me as I lay flat on my back on her kitchen floor.

"About fifteen minutes," she replied, her eyes darting anxiously around the kitchen.

I grabbed the corner of the counter and pulled myself upright, still a little woozy, my head feeling like it had been on the chisel end of a jackhammer. "What happened?" I asked, leaning over the kitchen sink. I turned the cold-water handle, splashing water on my face and the back of my neck.

"Some guy was hiding in one of the bedrooms. He came running out just as you turned around to leave; he hit you with some small, black object. Then he bolted out the front door."

I placed my hand on the back of my head. A small lump protruded just above the occipital bone. I grimaced when I put pressure on it. "Must have been a sap," I blurted out. I was rapidly coming to the conclusion that that's exactly how I felt.

"A what?" Becca asked.

"A sap. A short, weighted leather club. Did you get a look at him?" I asked, the lump on my head throbbing.

"I didn't see his face, Matt. He was wearing a mask, like one of those black ski masks."

I removed my cell phone from the inside pocket of my sports jacket and dialed 911. I sighed, shaking my head in response to the usual slew of irrelevant questions from the emergency dispatcher, stirred in with my report of what had happened. After identifying myself and the location a final time, she confirmed a detective would be dispatched. "MPD is on the way," I told Becca.

"Can I get you anything, Matt?" she asked.

"Appears you were right," I said, ignoring her question. "It also explains the missing notes. And he had every intention of leaving with them, which is why he slugged me from behind." I placed my hand on top of my throbbing head again, as if to emphasize the point.

Becca fidgeted nervously. "This is getting crazy," she blurted out. "Why would someone send threatening notes only to steal those same notes later?"

"That's for me to find out," I replied, my exasperated tone obvious. I was infuriated to the point I was now fully onboard with my investigation. The threatening notes, the apartment break-in, and now the knot on my head certainly appeared to corroborate the allegations made by my client. The doorbell rang, followed by loud knocking, then a shout of "Police."

"I'll answer it," I said, glancing at Becca and pushing myself away from the kitchen counter. I walked stealthily in the direction of a hallway separating the living room from the two bedrooms. I motioned for Becca to move further back into the kitchen, then positioned myself halfway around a dividing wall with only my left side visible. I gripped my short-barrel revolver firmly underneath my sports jacket, then shouted, "Door's open, come in," assuming the door remained unlocked after our unknown visitor bolted out earlier.

A uniformed officer slowly pushed the door inward, stepping cautiously inside. He could have been the poster child for alertness. His hand rested on top of his holstered service revolver.

"Someone call for the police?" he shouted again, followed by a second uniformed officer and a plainclothes female who I assumed was the detective.

"I did," I shouted back, releasing my grip on my gun and walking slowly into the open living room, my empty hands in plain view. "I'm Matt Duggan, Private Investigator," I continued in a normal tone.

"Did I hear someone say, *Matt Duggan*?" the plainclothes female asked, walking in my direction.

I glanced directly at her. She looked familiar. It was then I recognized her. "Officer Kate Blanchard, MPD?" I asked, referencing her previous position as a uniformed officer.

"That *was* me," she clarified. "Now it's Detective Sergeant Blanchard, with the 38th precinct. I knew your ex-partner, Seth McPherson. I was one of several officers on scene whenever Seth and his partner Leah Mulholland were called out on a homicide investigation; at least before she was implicated in his murder."

The light bulb clicked on. Kate Blanchard was a road patrol officer who was assigned to the 16th precinct several months after I retired and Mulholland took my place as Seth's partner. Seth had mentioned Blanchard on several occasions, stating more than once he would have preferred to have her as his new partner over the obnoxious Mulholland. Blanchard was bright and ambitious, with an intuitive nature that Seth believed would make for a good working chemistry. The problem was that Kate was new, a rookie, and even with his influence would not be able to overcome that hurdle. It would more than likely lead to a grievance complaint by Mulholland, one that Seth would lose. There was also the possibility of damage to Blanchard's reputation as a new officer, something Seth didn't want on his conscience.

I remember speaking briefly with Officer Blanchard on a few cases I worked with Seth as a private investigator after retiring from the MPD, and I understood why Seth liked her. As a new rookie, she would have to put in her time "on the beat" patrolling the streets, responding to calls and gathering information—standard operating procedure for a new uniformed officer.

"So, was it you who called for a detective?" she asked.

"On behalf of my client, that's a yes," I replied with a faint smile. I introduced Blanchard to Becca, then briefed her regarding the entire scenario, including the missing notes. She wrote on a small notepad, flipping it open and shut several times during our conversation and questioning before stuffing it back into her jacket.

"How's that bump on your noggin?" the detective inquired, moving closer for a better look. "Do you need medical attention?"

I shook my still-aching head. "No, I'm all right," I replied, refocusing on the matter at hand. I suggested a meeting with her and the state attorney. Placing the DA on notice might allow for an expanded search of criminal and civil public records, and any other confidential sources available that could shed light on the suspect law firm and their client pharmaceutical companies. Sergeant Blanchard agreed, stating she would contact me before the evening was over.

One of the uniformed officers approached. "We've checked out the entire apartment. Everything looks clean."

Blanchard turned and looked at Becca. "Anyone other than you and management have a key to the front door?"

"No," she answered, shaking her head nervously.

"Are you sure you locked both the door handle and deadbolt when you left for Matt's office?"

"Yes," Becca answered.

"There's no sign of a forced entry," Blanchard continued. "He either obtained or made a duplicate key, or jimmied the door handle lock and deadbolt." She looked at Matt, then glanced back at Becca. "If I were you, I'd find somewhere else to stay, at least for the time being."

I felt terrible for Becca. The sum of events had obviously taken its toll. She was a frightened wreck, and I couldn't say I blamed her. "I'll take care of that," I said, jumping in. I thanked the detective sergeant, adding a reminder I'd be waiting for her call later. She nodded, then led her two officers out the front door.

Becca walked slowly around the living room. She was quiet and contemplative. I didn't interrupt her. She needed a little time for everything to sink in. Finally, she walked up to me. "So, now that I'm officially in hiding, where do you suggest I go?"

I didn't hesitate. "You're staying with me," I replied firmly. "Gather what you need and we'll drive back to my office. I have a spare room upstairs and a guest bedroom in my home. You can use the room upstairs during the day and can stay in the spare room at my home in the evening. Delia will keep you company during the day while I conduct my investigation. If you need to go anywhere, Delia will go with you."

"Thank you for the offer, Matt, but I'm sure I'll be fine

here," Becca replied nervously, attempting to put on a brave front.

"I don't want any argument," I countered. "You're being intimidated and threatened. You've retained my services, and the other part of my job is to protect you, and that's exactly what I intend to do. Start packing."

"All right, all right," she said. Becca walked into her bedroom and pulled a suitcase out of her closet.

I carried her suitcase, a garment bag, and a few other items and placed everything in the trunk, then drove back to my agency. Delia helped settle Becca upstairs while I checked my email and phone messages. I was just finishing when my iPhone's screen illuminated with a call. It was Sergeant Blanchard.

"That was quick," I answered, not correlating her sooner than expected call with anything other than a confirmation of our pending meeting. "So, what time is our meeting with the state attorney tomorrow?"

"Forget the meeting," she snapped. "We've got another problem."

My gumshoe intuition kicked in, prompted by the tone of Blanchard's voice. I pushed my chair back and away from my desk, then stood. "Okay, I'm listening. What's the problem?"

"We just located someone who matches the description of the suspect who broke into your client's apartment earlier today."

"How's that a problem?" I asked, smiling. My mind was already busy conjuring up questions about the perp I assumed was in custody. I suppose I shouldn't have been surprised by her answer.

"He's dead."

PART III

As a private investigator, it's not unusual to run into the occasional detour. Unexpected twists, turns, and roadblocks are the norm. The more serious the crime, the greater the odds for additional foul play, up to and including murder. *Someone* wanted this guy silenced, worried he might let the cat out of the bag.

Blanchard was calling from her cell phone. I was keeping my fingers crossed that she was calling from the crime scene.

"I'm at the scene of the murder," she predictably revealed. "My officers and I have cordoned off the area. Another homicide detective is en route as well as crime scene techs and the coroner. He's definitely the guy who was in your client's apartment."

I sat back down in my chair, stunned. "Okay, just to clarify," I began, "you're telling me he matches the description of the guy who was in my client's apartment?"

"It's him."

"The perp who handed me a prescription for a sleeping pill on a stick?"

"Yes . . . again."

"You're absolutely sure?"

"Damnit Matt, that's yes three times now," she

snapped, her voice growing louder with each answer.

"How do you know?" I shouted back, unsure of her positive ID. "I was lights out, face down on the floor," I reminded Blanchard, while quickly recalling Becca's only view of this John Doe was his backside as he raced out the apartment door wearing a mask.

Sergeant Blanchard explained, "We found the so-called notes you mentioned when you briefed me at your client's apartment; it was pretty much verbatim as you described."

I grinned like I had just rolled three triple bars on a slot machine. "Yeah, it's definitely sounding like our guy, Detective. Where are you?" I asked, waiting for Blanchard to provide the location. My grin quickly disappeared when she answered.

"In front of your home."

* * *

By the time I arrived, it was dark, the entire neighborhood illuminated by the usual parade of flashing police and fire vehicles, ambulances, and news vans. The investigative team kept the media and other onlookers at a distance, securing the area with strategic placement of yellow crime scene tape and uniformed officers patrolling the front of the property. My backyard was fenced, the media and onlookers warned to remain at a distance. I exited my vehicle and quickly walked toward a uniformed officer standing at the end of my driveway, my bifold ID wallet in hand and opened to display my license and badge.

"Let him through," Blanchard shouted at the officer as she exited the front door of my house, waving a latex-gloved hand and walking in my direction. Arriving home to the circus in progress outside my house felt eerily surreal, and it didn't help that I now needed permission to walk onto my own property. I stooped slightly to move under the tape the officer raised. As soon as I stood upright, Blanchard took me aside and brought me up to speed; she was not a happy camper.

"We responded to a 911 dispatch of gunfire. Your neighbor across the street noticed an adult male running down your driveway toward a waiting car parked next to the curb in front of your house. He jumped in the right front seat and the car shot out of there like a rocket-propelled grenade; that same neighbor ran across the street and up the separate walkway. That's when he discovered the deceased face down behind the hedges next to the house just outside the front door; we're in the process of attempting to identify him. He had no wallet or ID, so we'll have to rely on finger-prints, or DNA if no prints are in the database."

"Was he in my home?"

"We believe he was—the door was ajar when we arrived. He used a picklock set we found in his pocket, probably the same one he used to gain entry into your client's apartment."

I poked my head inside the door; nothing appeared out of the ordinary that I could see, although I knew I would need to go inside for a more thorough look around.

"It appears he was shot outside of your house," Blanchard said.

My mind was racing. *What the hell was he doing in my home?* I thought to myself, finally pushing the front door inward and walking inside. I completed a quick visual of my one-story bungalow, coming to the same conclusion as Blanchard: Nothing caught my immediate attention. I walked back outside as the culprit's body was being placed on a gurney for transport to the coroner's office.

"It was a 9mm," Blanchard revealed, holding a clear sandwich-size baggie with three expended copper shell casings inside. She handed the baggie back to one of the crime scene techs to be placed with other evidence gathered, then reached down and picked up a small brown paper bag and opened it. "I almost forget," she continued, "this is the sap we found on the deceased—probably the same one used to put that knot on the back of your head."

I gave a quick nod, pursed my lips in frustration, and turned around. I wanted to go back inside my house and examine it more thoroughly, but decided to wait until MPD's investigation was complete. It was obvious now, at least to me, that someone at Becca's former law firm not only wanted return of the incriminating notes, but elimination of the designated henchman as well—*add murder to the shopping list.* There was no longer any doubt that Becca's life was in danger, and I was even more determined to find the ringleader behind it. Evidence continued to mount toward a cabal of crooked attorneys and greedy pharmaceutical executives, their motive wealth and influence facilitated by skirting federal and state regulations limiting the amount of opioids legally allowed to be produced and marketed.

"You okay?" Blanchard inquired, her question interrupting my train of thought. I turned in her direction.

"I believe it's time to involve the feds," I replied, ignoring her question as I stared directly into her steely gray eyes.

"You mean the DEA?"

"And the FBI," I replied. "We've got a law firm and one or more pharmaceutical companies involved in a murder and criminal conspiracy."

"We're almost done here," she responded obliquely. "Meet me at the state attorney's office tomorrow morning at nine. Bring your client with you."

* * *

An hour later, the last MPD and rescue vehicles departed. I turned and strolled casually on the concrete walkway toward the front door. I wanted to take another look at the inside of my home, then drive back to my office to check on Becca and Delia; that's when I heard my name being called.

"Matt . . . Hey, Matt," a voice said from behind, catching my attention.

I stopped and turned around. It was my neighbor from across the street. "Hey Jim," I answered hurriedly as he walked in my direction. James O'Malley was the typical conscientious, watchful neighbor who always noticed when a non-resident or unfamiliar vehicle made its way into the neighborhood. He knew what I did for a living, so he had been on full alert when he heard what he believed to be gunfire, then noticed the driver-occupied four-door sedan, idling roughly and parked in front of my home.

"I ran across the street just as some dude jumped into the front seat of the waiting car. As soon as the door shut, the driver floored it. I continued up the walkway, and that's when I noticed the guy face down behind the hedges. He wasn't breathing. I checked for a pulse—nothing. That's when the first police and emergency vehicles arrived."

My watchful neighbor was fidgeting, rubbing his chin and looking around. He was clearly irked about something. He stuck his hands in the pockets of his light jacket.

"I was questioned by the first two officers, and later by Sergeant Blanchard and another detective. I told them both the same thing I just told you, then her partner told me to take a hike—said he had everything he needed from me—so I walked back to my house and sat in the garage. A few minutes later you showed up. I was waiting for them to leave so we could talk."

I didn't have time nor was I in the mood to give a thank-you speech about how much I appreciated my neighbor's crime prevention efforts, nor apologize for the rudeness of the unknown detective. I would thank him later. It appeared he knew something and wanted my private audience.

"Okay, Jim, you have my attention. What is it you want to tell me?"

"Well, I would have told that detective if he hadn't been such a dick," he fired back.

I laughed. "That's what they used to call us," referring to the word *dick*, a dated, shortened version of the word detective. I'm sure he knew what I meant, but I wasn't in the mood, and I didn't have time to clarify. He just admitted he knew something, and I needed that information. "Okay, Jim, let's have it."

"Can you tell me what this is all about, Matt?" His question caught me off guard. "Just out of curiosity?" he asked, a wry smile on his face.

I sighed. Not that it was any of his business—it wasn't. He was overstepping his boundaries as a watchful neighbor. "You know I can't divulge any information regarding my client or the case," I reminded him. "Now, for the last time, what is it?"

He paused for a moment, then gave a cheesy grin. "I wrote down the license plate number on that car."

PART IV

I'm running late, I thought to myself, a reminder to slow down as I sped back to the office. Although it was well past normal working hours, I knew Delia would still be around to keep Becca company, to include a meal order delivery due to the extended hours. I called the office and brought Delia up to speed on what occurred at my home, then provided the plate number of the getaway vehicle that my neighbor recorded.

"I'll have this processed before you arrive," she assured me.

I pulled into the office complex and parked, exited my vehicle, and scurried toward the front door. The office lights shimmered softly through the opaque window film applied to the vertical sidelights of the main office doorway. I reached for the doorknob, then hesitated. Call it a sixth sense, a gut feeling, intuition . . . something just didn't feel right.

I unlocked the door, then gave it a gentle push, moving inward in unison with the door as it slowly opened. "Delia, Becca?" I called out softly.

No response.

I removed my revolver from its holster, then remained motionless, detecting no sound or movement.

I continued inside, noticing Delia's desk was vacant, her chair shoved back against the wall. My office door was closed. I carefully opened the door, flicking on the light switch. My chair was turned around, facing the window behind my desk. It took only seconds to realize Delia was in the chair. She was bound and gagged so tightly she couldn't move or utter a sound. I placed my gun back into its holster, then proceeded to remove the gag. Her eyes widened the moment the cloth dropped below her chin.

"Matt, behind you!" she yelled.

I turned and instinctively jumped back and away from the unmistakable click of a switchblade or stiletto, its spring-loaded blade locking into position. I was facing an unknown male, dressed in a pair of worn jeans, a long-sleeve pullover shirt, and a ski mask pulled down to his chin. He was in a knife-fighting stance, lurching forward, jabbing and swinging a glistening, black-handled knife. I moved clockwise, dodging his attack, my back against the wall. The knife-wielding thug continued after me until I reached my coat valet. I grabbed the coat rack and slammed it between his outstretched and widened arms. The thick metal pole struck the perp in the forehead, stunning him; he wobbled slightly, then dropped to his knees. I stepped slightly to my right and connected with a stinging haymaker to the left side of his head; he crumpled and slumped unconscious on his left side. I reached down and grabbed the knife.

Delia appeared rattled, but uninjured. "You're bleeding, Matt," she said, still tied to the chair.

"Where's Becca?" I asked, ignoring her observation. I used the hoodlum's knife to cut the rope binding Delia, then helped her to her feet.

"This guy and his partner walked in half an hour before you arrived," she began. "They were wearing ski masks, both carrying guns." Delia pointed to the thug on the floor. "This creep gagged and then tied me to your chair. His partner zip-tied Becca and placed duct tape over her mouth, then forced her out the door. I heard tires squealing, so the other guy must have thrown her in their car and left, but not before I heard Prince Charming here tell his sidekick, 'I'll take care of Duggan when he gets back.'"

I removed a spare handkerchief from my desk drawer and wrapped it around my hand, then grabbed the telephone receiver and called Blanchard. "I'm on my way," she replied after I briefed her regarding the incident in my office.

I placed the receiver back on its cradle, then turned and glanced at Delia. "Are you sure you're okay?"

She looked at me, agitation written all over her face. "Let me see your hand, Matt," she ordered, avoiding my question. She placed her hand under my wrist, then unwrapped the handkerchief. "Looks like he nicked you pretty good, right in the snuffbox below your thumb. Let me grab the first aid kit."

"Not before I secure this bozo," I retorted, turning our "visitor" face down, restraining him with handcuffs Delia removed from my desk drawer. I grabbed the unconscious assailant under the armpits, pulling and twisting him into a sitting position. I dragged him out of my office and propped him against a group of file cabinets in the main lobby.

I checked his pockets. I walked to the bathroom and washed my hands after leaving a trail of blood on the floor and the perp's clothing. "No wallet, no ID," I told Delia as I exited, drying my hands with a paper towel and using it as a bandage.

She opened a file cabinet and removed the office first aid bag, unzipping it on my desk. Delia cleaned and disinfected the laceration, covering it with a gauze dressing. She used just enough micropore tape to hold it in place.

I looked over my bandaged hand. "Nice job."

Delia glanced at me, smiling while she counted and placed the contents of the first aid supplies back into the red-zippered case. Let's see, that's one package of gauze, one roll of tape, one . . ." She stopped her count in response to the hoodlum groaning and regaining consciousness.

"Ahh! O-oh! Ugh!" the perp moaned, lifting his head upright and opening his eyes. He looked up at Delia, smiling in an irritatingly smug way.

"Oh, and here's one for you—you bastard," Delia shouted, dropping the first aid supplies and kneeing her assailant solidly in the jaw. His head slumped forward again, his chin resting on his chest.

* * *

"What's with Sleeping Beauty?" Blanchard asked, exchanging glances with Delia and me, the unconscious suspect motionless as she walked through the door. Two uniformed officers accompanied her. "And what happened to your hand?"

"He insisted on catching a few winks while waiting for you to show up," I sneered, snatching the switchblade off the desk corner and pressing the release button. Blanchard jerked her head toward the sound of the spring-loaded blade popping into position.

"That answers my second question." She motioned for her two officers to take a position on either side of the perp. "Help this guttersnipe off the floor and set him in that chair," she ordered, pointing. "Do you have any smelling salts in that first aid kit?"

Delia reached into the bag and removed an ammonia

ampoule, handing it to Blanchard. She snapped it open, then waved it in front of the unconscious man's nose. He reflexively moved his head up, twitching back and forth and away from the ammonia vapor. He opened his eyes, then flailed his arms, trying to push the capsule away. "The lights are back on," Blanchard quipped.

"All right, champ, start talking. Who are you and where's the other girl who was here?" I demanded.

"I was just doing what I was told," the injured thug garbled, bobbing his head, still groggy from my punch and Delia's knee to the chin. "My jaw—I think it's broken," he mumbled.

"He's not going to talk, Matt," Kate said. "We'll book him on breaking and entering, kidnapping and assault, and attempted murder—that's after we take him to the hospital. His jaw does appear to be broken."

"She did it," the crook garbled, turning his head and looking upward at Delia.

"Oh, really? *Prove it*," Blanchard replied, her tone mocking. She motioned her two officers to walk toward her and the gangster wannabe. "Help him out of the chair," she said.

The MPD officers stood on either side of the suspect, then reached down to lift him out of the chair. "On your feet," one of the officers ordered, the perp wobbling slightly as he was assisted upright.

Blanchard read the culprit his rights, then directed her officers to place him in the back seat of the cruiser. "Drop by the precinct early tomorrow, Matt. We'll have Mr. Mysterious identified before you arrive. You and Delia should get some rest. Oh, and remind me to return your cuffs."

I nodded. "What about Becca?"

"That's exactly what our line of questioning will focus

on, just as soon as he's done at the hospital and we complete his booking at MPD. And we'll do it with pen and paper if his stupid pie hole is wired shut."

I smirked. "I'll see you at the precinct in the morning."

Blanchard and her officers walked out of the agency with the cuffed suspect in tow. They placed him in the backseat of their cruiser and left for the hospital. I closed and locked the door, then pulled the shade down, covering the door's decorative glass panel. I turned and walked toward my assistant's desk.

"I'm scared to death for Becca," Delia said. "Unless that perp talks, MPD can't do a thing about her whereabouts."

I didn't disagree with her assessment. "Did you run the plate number that I gave you over the phone?"

Delia smiled. "I did you one better. I ran the plate *and* a criminal history. The owner's been a busy beaver—talk about a rap sheet. His crooked past looks like a road map." Delia opened her middle drawer and picked up the folded copies, handing them to me.

"Yeah, about the length of the entire country," I confirmed, chewing on my bottom lip as I perused over the folded printouts. I looked up at my assistant. "Thanks, this is exactly what I need."

Delia gave a sidelong glance. "Uh, Matt," she began cautiously, "are you planning what I think you're planning?"

I chuckled—she knew me too well, including why I didn't say anything to Blanchard about the printouts. The MPD detective had enough on her plate as it was, and I had no intention of risking Becca's life with any further delays. It was obvious after reviewing the printout that the perps who terrorized Delia and kidnapped Becca were the same two who shot and killed their colleague outside of my home, one of them now in custody and the other with Becca in tow.

"You're going after her, aren't you?" Delia knowingly asked.

I responded with a rhetorical glare.

"Well, I'm going with you," Delia announced tersely. "You're not doing this solo again," she continued, scouring through her desk, grabbing a can of mace, zip ties, and another pair of handcuffs.

"NO!" I fired back.

"Matt!" she bellowed in frustration. "It's too risky."

I looked at Delia appreciatively, walking over to her, gently placing my hands on top of her shoulders. "Hey, you've been through enough today—which is exactly why you're *not* going. As a matter of fact—"

"No, I'm *not* going home," she interrupted. "Not until I hear back from you."

I smiled and winked, then grabbed my sports jacket. I turned around and headed for the door, printouts in hand. "I'll be in touch," I told her, walking out of the office.

Delia paused, then walked up to the door, peeking through the shade, watching until Matt drove out of the office complex parking lot. She turned and walked back to her desk, grabbing her handbag. Stuffing her cuffs, mace, iPhone, zip ties, and handheld taser inside, she turned again and walked back to the door. "He'll just have to fire me."

PART V

The DMV printout confirmed the suspect vehicle was a Mercury Cougar owned by Adam Booth, a known thug with a record the length of a landfill, and just as dirty. His separate arrest record validated a history of petty theft beginning at age fourteen, the nature of those offenses gradually escalating all the way to attempted murder. By age thirty-four, he had firmly established himself as a career criminal, with an additional history of juvenile detention, city and county jail bookings that would make attorney Johnnie Cochran envious. Recently paroled from Iron Port Regional Prison for bank robbery, he wasted no time offering his services to the highest bidder.

I drove in the direction the GPS voice directed, my iPhone positioned on the lower dash, just in front of the shift knob. *A few more minutes and I should be there.*

The neighborhood appeared to be an older community of working-class single-family houses, apparent from the worn-out roofs, paint-hungry homes, and disheveled yards crying out for needed maintenance. Cars were parked unevenly in driveways and in a staggered array on the swale between the sidewalk and street.

Idling slowly down the asphalt-paved road, I squinted to compensate for the darkened neighborhood. It was then the GPS announced, "You have reached your destination."

I stopped the car, searching for a house number on a mailbox or visible part of the home. Before any numbers came into view, a vehicle matching the DMV description began to back out of a one-car driveway two houses ahead. I moved my foot off the brake pedal, my car idling slowly forward again until the headlights illuminated the vehicle's rear tag. It was a match. The suspect vehicle continued to exit out of the driveway, turning sharply until the rear of the car was less than a foot away from a neighboring fire hydrant. *I've got him.* I gunned the engine, quickly maneuvering my car in front of the perp's vehicle. I jumped out and raced to the driver's side window with my gun drawn.

"Both hands on the wheel," I shouted at the startled driver, the surprised suspect immediately complying. I reached for the door handle, tugging the latch and slowly pulling the door open. "Step out of the car, *Booth.*"

It was just enough commotion to mask the quiet footfall that followed. A dark clothed figure suddenly approached me from behind. "Don't move," the accomplice whisper-shouted—a voice that sounded oddly familiar. "Drop the gun—hands behind your head. Now back away from the door, nice and slow."

Booth exited the Cougar, a satisfying smirk playing across his face. He slowly stooped to retrieve my dropped revolver, gradually returning to an upright position. "Turn around," he said.

I reluctantly complied with the perp's order, taking my time and slowly turning in the opposite direction. Completing the about-face, I strolled a gaze over my captor. Resignation over the current situation vanished, replaced by an expression of total shock.

A wicked smirk made its way across the face of the driver's accomplice. "Cat got your tongue?" A sarcastic snarl accompanied the question.

I stood, staring . . . baffled, until the only word to come to mind crossed my lips. "*Becca?*" I turned in response to the movement of her partner, just in time to see a gun come crashing down on my skull.

* * *

"OKAY, WAKE UP. Let's go. C'mon, get out of there."

I heard myself moan as I opened my eyes, peering up at Booth and Becca, the darkness of night surrounding them.

"Don't make me tell you again," Booth shouted.

I quickly looked around. The smell of the musty trunk and spare tire confirmed my initial thoughts—I was inside the trunk of the same car I had blocked earlier. *Shit, how the hell did this happen?* I tried to sit up, pushing with my hands tied at the wrists behind me. My head felt like a wrecking ball, lightning bolts of pain bouncing back and forth inside my skull.

"Help him out of the trunk." Booth gestured to Becca, stepping away from the vehicle.

"Your arm broken?" Becca sneered.

"I don't want any problems. And I'm the one holding the gun, remember?"

"His hands are tied behind his back, what—"

"Shut up and help him out of the trunk like I told ya," Booth fired back.

Becca reached down and placed her hands around my upper arm, pulling as I hooked my legs over the top of the trunk. With her help I finally scooted over the top, landing unsteadily on a hard surface of what appeared to be multi-shaped decorative pavers.

A driveway, I thought, my head still throbbing.

"Start walking," Booth ordered, waving the gun toward the front of the car.

Her hands still wrapped around my arm, Becca prompted me to walk along the pavers in the direction indicated by Booth. A near-full moon provided the only illumination, the dim lunar light straining to filter its way through the surrounding trees and shrubbery.

"Keep going," Booth ordered, walking behind Becca and me.

Moving along until we reached an opening in the surrounding vegetation, I caught a glimpse of a huge, two-story dwelling. It looked new, like it was recently completed, a small mansion purposely built in the middle of at least ten or more surrounding acres. The enveloping darkness and dim exterior lighting made it appear drab, as if the painters had forgotten to apply the mandatory layer of color to it. There was a detached garage approximately twenty-five yards to the right of the main building.

"Park it in front of the garage," Booth yelled out.

I trudged obliquely in the direction of the three-car garage, then leaned with my back against a garage door. My hands and wrists ached from being tightly bound. Grimacing, I looked over at Booth. "Okay, so what's the story?"

Ignoring my question, Booth handed the revolver to Becca. He reached inside his sports jacket, removing a cell phone. "Make sure our Dick Tracy wannabe doesn't go anywhere," he ordered. "I'll be back in a few minutes."

Booth turned and walked hurriedly toward the front of the house, tapping the keypad of the cell phone as he walked.

Certain he was out of earshot, I turned and rendered a

hard stare at Becca. "I can't wait to hear your side of this."

"You'll hear *my* side soon enough," Becca shot back. "Be quiet. I hear someone coming."

Booth returned, walking around the corner of the garage with another male. He appeared middle aged, with graying hair and a neatly trimmed mustache. He was sporting a dark suit, a red-and-black striped necktie, and matching wingtips. "So, is this the infamous *Matt Duggan, Private Investigator*?" he asked while grinning, looking directly at me.

One of the ringleaders, I thought, returning the suited man's stare. "Sounds like a rhetorical question," I snickered. "You figure it out, genius."

The impeccably dressed man exchanged his grin for a frown. "Take him down to the basement. We'll decide what to do with him later."

Booth took the gun from Becca. Looking at Matt, he waved the pistol, then pointed with his other hand. "Move," he barked.

I began walking in the direction of the mansion, Becca and Booth behind me. I craned my neck at the sound of a garage door opening, catching a glimpse of several cars parked inside.

"I'll be back in half an hour, maybe sooner," the mustached male said to Booth, walking toward one of the vehicles. He pointed and pressed his key fob button, the car of his choice blinking in response.

* * *

It's a miracle I didn't lose that creep, Delia thought, having followed Booth's vehicle earlier. She remained parked on the darkened shoulder off the road. She let out a short sigh as she watched a Mercedes emerge out of the thick covering of trees, turning in the opposite direction and onto the main highway where it connected with the paved driveway.

She exited the car with her cell phone and followed the pavers, spotting the small mansion and Booth's car after walking approximately seventy-five yards. No sooner had she arrived at the garage, the faint vision of vehicle lights began to reflect off the front of both buildings. She quickly made her way to a vantage point around the back, a parade of stylish and expensive vehicles turning left at the fork and stopping on the circular driveway in front of the main house.

Male and female occupants began exiting the parked cars. Men and women in business suits or formal attire followed one another to the front door of the mansion, greeted by a male and female butler.

Inside, they were led to a large conference room, then seated around a twenty-five-foot-long boat-shaped table. Bottled water, ice, soda, tea, coffee, snacks, and condiments were available on large portable carts at each end of the room. A state-of-the-art video conferencing system was in place, along with two speaker phones evenly spaced along the length of the table. A linen-covered journal was placed in front of every seat, documents placed inside to coincide with the meeting.

The attendees had sufficient time to indulge. They moved in the direction of their seats when a formally attired middle-age male and female not part of the original party entered the room. The male glanced at a large, digital clock centered near the top of the wall on the opposite end of the room. It was exactly ten p.m.

"Good evening," the man announced, raising the

volume of his voice so he could be heard over the chatter in the room. "Please be seated."

* * *

Directing me down a winding staircase with a curt reminder to Becca to open the door when we reached the bottom, Booth placed his free hand between my shoulder blades and abruptly shoved me through the opened door. "Make sure he doesn't cause any trouble," he instructed Becca, handing her my revolver again. He stopped and turned around, preparing to return upstairs.

"Where are you going?" she asked Booth.

"Conference room security. I'll be back later."

Closing and locking the door, Becca turned and faced me, pointing my gun at me. "Sit down," she ordered, pointing the gun at a worn-wedge arm sofa in the middle of the room. It was an unfinished basement with bare walls, a small table and chairs, a half-bath and wet bar. There was a closed door on the far side wall. The interior of the basement was barely discernible; a small low-wattage lamp on top of the sofa's end table provided the only illumination.

My wrists and hands were numb. My shoulders ached from the tension. "Before I sit," I bellowed angrily, "just tell me one thing: *why*?"

Becca turned and locked eyes with me, her face full of fury. "*Why*?" she mimicked sarcastically. "You really want to know *why*?" she repeated louder. Smirking, she sauntered slowly toward me, walking behind and around me in an intimidating manner. She pressed and ran the end of the gun barrel down the side of my face. Noticing no reaction, she took a step back, then lowered the weapon, allowing it to rest against her hip.

I flashed a cheeky grin. "Well, I'm waiting," I taunted her, followed by a wink.

Becca's facial expression resumed its previous fury; she raised the gun until it was pointed at me, then immediately stiffened as the crackling sound of a taser echoed throughout the room. Three seconds of firm contact on the left side of Becca's exposed neck was all that was needed; loss of balance, muscle control, mental confusion, and disorientation followed—she dropped like a ragdoll. The gun slipped out of her hand and onto the basement floor.

"I barely noticed your wink," Delia said as she stooped down and zip-tied Becca, still squirming and moaning on the exposed cement floor.

"Talk about timing—you must be psychic," I said, exhaling a sigh of relief.

Delia acknowledged with a smile, then noticed a cleaning rag next to a can of paint on the floor near the wet bar; she grabbed it and tore off a long strip before securing a gag tightly around Becca's mouth. She dragged her toward the wet bar, then used the remaining rag to tie her to an exposed plumbing pipe behind the counter. Delia quietly pulled the wet bar's two drawers open, finding a small, serrated utensil knife. She walked back to me and cut the nylon rope binding my wrists; she rubbed my hands until sensation began to return.

"How did you get in?" I asked, grimacing as I gained enough feeling to continue the massage on my own.

Delia went on to explain the procession of cars and SUVs that rolled in, parking in front of the mansion along with the twelve people exiting the vehicles and entering the dwelling. I listened, bending down and retrieving my revolver.

"I remained out of sight behind the detached garage until everyone in that motorcade walked through the double front door. I ran from the garage to the back of the main dwelling. I started looking for a way in when I noticed a rectangular awning window at ground level. I have similar basement windows at my home; they're hinged at the top and swing open toward the inside. I had to jimmy the window a bit, but I managed to open it and let myself in."

"How did you know I was in the basement?"

Delia gave a half-smile. "Remind me to tell you later. Blanchard and a SWAT team are on their way," she continued. "The guy she took to the hospital spilled his guts before his jaw was wired shut. I called her while I was behind the garage. I gave her as much info on this location as I could."

I nodded. "That must be the main basement entry," I said, pointing to a set of French doors that were accessible via a concrete step-up inside the room. "Looks like they lead to the back of the—"

I was interrupted by the sound of the interior upstairs basement door being unlocked. I glanced at Delia. "Try and keep her quiet," I whispered, placing my hand on Delia's shoulder and directing her toward Becca. I stood erect, my back against a dividing wall around the corner at the bottom of the stairway. I raised my handgun until it was level with my temple.

"Becca?" Booth called out as he began to walk down the stairs. He slowed the pace of his descent when she didn't respond, then stopped. Continuing again, he removed a pistol tucked into his waistband. Both feet on the smooth concrete, Booth turned in response to what he thought was mumbling. I wheeled around the corner of the stairway, bringing the butt end of my revolver down on the back of Booth's head, dropping him like a bad transmission.

"Nappy time for you, bucko."

PART VI

I walked around the front of the syndicate's top minion, bending down and initiating a fireman's carry, lifting and draping the unconscious perp over my shoulder and walking in the direction of the sofa. "Grab that chair, Delia, or whatever it is, and pull it away from the sofa."

She quickly moved the nostalgic shaker toward the center of the basement. I lowered Booth in a sitting position in the antique chair. Delia removed a pair of handcuffs draped around her belt in the small of her back, pulled Booth's hands behind him, and cuffed his wrists around the chair's beefy back post.

I picked up the nylon rope used earlier to bind my hands in the back of Booth's car. There was enough remaining to secure Booth's ankles to the legs of his new seat. "That should keep him out of our hair while I deal with those corporate crooks upstairs," I mumbled, giving an angry glance at the door atop the stairway.

Delia found another rag on the floor, tearing off an amount sufficient to keep the cabal's primary enforcer quiet should he regain consciousness. "There, that should do it," she grunted quietly, tying the gag's final knot around the back of Booth's head. She took a step back, then felt the vibration of her cell phone. Removing the device from her back pocket, she tapped in the privacy code. It was a text from Sergeant Blanchard.

"What's the message?" I asked, noticing the phone's illumination.

"It's Blanchard," Delia replied, looking directly at Matt. "A SWAT team is on the way, along with a half-dozen DEA agents."

A quick smile. "Let's see if we can make it easier for them." I handed Booth's gun to Delia. "Keep an eye on these two while I mosey on upstairs; they're probably still in the conference room—that should make it easy to get the drop on them."

Delia nodded. "Be careful, Matt."

Holding my revolver, I walked slowly up the staircase until I reached the door. I grabbed and turned the doorknob, pushing it just enough until I could see into the hallway. *So far, so good.* I stepped into the passageway leading to several other rooms, quietly walking toward the sound of a male's voice through the door at the end of the long corridor.

"Everything is ready," I heard the unknown male announce to the attendees. "Veritas, Plexus, and Theta Pharmaceuticals will be ramping up their production quotas within the week. My senior partners and I want to assure you, our clients, that our team of dedicated associates are especially adept at corporate, administrative, regulatory, and marketing law. They have all the necessary connections, all the correct middlemen, government and corporate officials in their pockets. In the event of any roadblocks, our people are fully prepared to employ their legal knowledge and experience to include inadequacies and ambiguities in the law, if needed; in other words, and if necessary, they can circumvent the entire regulatory system." He paused for a moment before adding, "In essence, ladies and gentlemen, we're ready to meet the exponential demand of our growing customer base."

Sounds like all the major players are present; this could be the pot of gold at the end of the rainbow. Blanchard and her people should be here any moment. I placed my hand on the doorknob and turned it slowly. In a split second, I pushed the door open and bolted through the opening.

"Nobody move," I shouted, holding my snub-nose revolver in an upright position.

The startled attendees all turned their heads in my direction. Several appeared frightened as kids at a Halloween horror show. In an instant, their expressions confirmed the meeting was over, like an angry boss deciding the meeting was a waste of time and sending everyone back to their cubicles. No one would be leaving tonight with a smile on their face.

"Where the hell did you come from?" the main speaker asked, caught off guard by my sudden appearance. He moved away from the mahogany podium, pushing the flexible microphone aside before turning and walking aggressively in my direction.

Using my free hand, I delivered a thunderous left hook to the right side of the dumbfounded speaker's face, driving him backward past the podium and onto the floor. He literally slid into the corner on his end of the room.

"I'm Matt Duggan, remember? We met earlier by the garage—now pick your crooked ass off the floor and have a seat at the conference table," I snarled, leaning against the podium with a satisfied smirk. "We'll be joined by some special guests shortly."

* * *

"Nice job," Sergeant Blanchard said, offering her congratulations. "I'll have to admit it was a pleasant surprise seeing you waiting at the door, inviting us inside. We normally have to break it down with a ramming bar," she chuckled, standing next to Delia and me in the dining area just outside the conference room.

"You can add Booth and Becca to the list," I said. "Delia walked them both upstairs from the basement just before you arrived; they're in the conference room as well. She kept a watchful eye over the entire family while I observed you and your people roll up on us."

Blanchard acknowledged with a half-smile. "They're all under arrest. The SWAT team has secured the home, including the grounds outside. The butlers were attempting to flee and were taken into custody. The state attorney and federal prosecutor's office completed a preliminary investigation of the law firm, uncovering evidence of a link with the pharmaceutical companies; production quota discrepancies were noted as well. That was the smoking gun we needed to obtain the appropriate warrants. The DEA and FBI will now begin their interrogations and investigation, along with anything else we find."

"Well, if they're as smart as they all think they are, they'll shut up and lawyer up. You'll probably he here as long as it takes to complete your search of the premises before carting them all off to the big house. And before I forget, I would advise you to seize the entire—"

Blanchard interrupted. "Yes, I know—the video conference system. We're on it. That will be dismantled and brought back to the appropriate forensics lab for investigation and reconstruction."

The lead DEA agent walked up to Blanchard. "Just thought you'd like to know the senior partners for Colby,

Miller & Wright—they're all present," he said with a smirk.

Matt and Blanchard exchanged glances.

"Oh, as well as the CEOs, CFOs, and COOs of all three pharmaceutical companies," the agent went on, exchanging his smirk for a wide grin. Turning to me, he added, "That guy you clobbered—he's the original founder of the firm, the head honcho, Mr. Miller himself."

I let out a chuckle.

"Still, something puzzles me," Blanchard chimed in. "What's Becca's role in all of this? She came to you originally playing the victim, only to find out she's as involved and up to her neck as the rest of her colleagues. Did you get anything out of her?"

I looked at Delia. "Did she say anything while you were downstairs with her and Booth?"

Delia shook her head. "No, she remained gagged until the SWAT team took her into custody."

I turned and looked at Blanchard. "Mind if I talk to Becca . . . alone?"

"Knock yourself out. Nobody's going anywhere for a while."

I walked over to Becca, still sitting at the far end of the conference room. Her chair was pushed up against the table, her head bent forward, starring downward at the tabletop. She was quiet, obviously upset, not wanting to engage with anyone.

"Becca," I called out to her softly. She raised her head slightly, craning her neck in my direction. "Come with me, please. I'd like to talk to you."

I carefully helped her out of her chair, guiding her by the elbow. Blanchard directed the DEA agent to remove her handcuffs. I walked Becca out of the conference hall and into an adjoining room. Several small folding chairs were leaning against a wall. I grabbed two, unfolded both, and placed them on the floor facing each other.

"Please have a seat," I politely asked. Becca quietly complied, sitting in one of the chairs.

"I know you want me to talk," Becca began, "but you won't believe anything I say, so why bother," she sobbed, tears streaming down her face.

"Try me."

She hesitated. "I feel absolutely horrible, so terribly ashamed. I can't even look you in the face," she cried, turning away.

I placed my hand on Becca's chin, gently turning her face back toward mine. "Becca, you were my client . . . not once, but twice, and as far as I'm concerned, a friend as well. Talk to me."

Sobbing, she cried out, "They were going to kill you, Matt. The senior partners were fearful you would succeed in uncovering enough evidence that it would lead to their arrests and a shutdown of the firm. With you and your investigation out of the way, they believed they could litigate or defend their way around state and federal author- ities. I learned about this after Booth abducted me out of your office. They told me I'd get a pass if I cooperated, my first task that of luring *you* into a position to be abducted. They figured you'd come after me, and it worked. I agreed to it, but it was only a ploy—just to get you here, then take advantage of their trust to somehow allow you to get the information regarding the meeting and location to the authorities. It was their intention to dispose of you after the meeting."

"You knew this meeting was scheduled?"

"Yes, but only after I agreed to play ball and assure them of my sincerity."

"You were very convincing down in the basement. I really believed you were going to blow my brains out."

"I had to be convincing—they had to know I was believable; they were watching me even when I didn't think they were," Becca confessed, continuing to cry. "I was only seconds away from untying you and revealing it was all just a ruse; that's when Delia tagged me with the taser."

I sighed, pursed my lips, then stood. I helped Becca to her feet. She leaned into me, hugging me tightly. "I'm so sorry," she wept.

I stepped back and removed my pocket square, handing it to my client.

"What's going to happen to me?" she asked.

I placed my hands on her shoulders. "The first thing you need to do is go back into the conference room and cooperate with Blanchard and the DEA. I'll talk with Blanchard later and make her aware of our conversation. Hire competent legal counsel if you wish, but from here on your dealings with everyone involved are to be nothing less than open and transparent—understood?"

"Understood," Becca replied, nodding in agreement.

I grinned. "It's nice to see a smile on that beautiful face again."

* * *

"I don't see any reason for you two to hang around," Blanchard informed Delia and me outside the conference room. "We'll take into consideration the conversation you had with Becca. You two call it a night. We'll be in touch. We have a lot to sort out."

"No argument here," I said, glancing at Blanchard, then my assistant. "Del and I have a bit of sorting out to do as well."

Delia returned a puzzled gaze, then looked at Blanchard, shrugging.

* * *

As we walked back to Delia's car, an awkward silence followed. She pressed the open trunk button on her key fob, then reached inside, grabbing her purse. She strolled to the driver's side of her car, then stood.

"You plan on opening the door?"

Delia sighed. "We need to talk, Matt. I know when something's bothering you; you're not one to hold back. What is it?"

I continued around the front of the car toward the driver's side. I folded my arms and leaned against the rear door. After a short pause, I provided a quick summary of my conversation with Becca.

"Do you believe her?" Delia asked.

"I don't know," I said, "and that's what bothers me. I didn't share that doubt with Blanchard when I spoke with her later. And I'm reminded I almost lost my license the first time I took on Becca as a client."

"Is that the 'sorting out' you were referring to?" Delia asked.

I unfolded my arms and moved away from the car. Turning and looking at my assistant, I smiled. "Hey, remember when I asked you how you knew I was in the basement, and you said you'd tell me later?"

Delia paused. "Yes," she replied, realizing I was avoiding the question.

"Well, let's have it. How did you know?"

Delia gave a mischievous smile. "Reach into the left

outside pocket of your jacket."

"Do what?" I asked.

"Go on, reach into the left pocket of your jacket," she repeated.

I reached inside. I felt a small, button-like object. I looked up at Delia as I wrapped my hand around a small, circular item and removed it. Opening my hand, I immediately recognized it was a coin-size GPS tracker pad.

I looked at the tracking device for only a moment, then directly at Delia. "I oughta fire you!" I yelled, unable to maintain an angry face for more than a few seconds. She had saved my life—again.

Delia turned and looked at me, another impish smirk appearing.

"And wipe that silly grin off your face—you look like the Cheshire cat. When did you . . . ?"

"Can we talk about it over an early breakfast?" Delia interrupted, walking up to me and threading her hands around my arm, pulling me away from the car.

I chuckled. "You're driving."

THE END

THE CASE OF THE MISSING VIRUS

EPISODE III

PROLOGUE

Private Investigator Matt Duggan is hired to locate a missing scientist involved in bioweapons research. To complicate matters, two vials of a deadly virus are also reported missing. Working in tandem with the FBI, Matt and his assistant begin their investigation only to find themselves as unwilling subjects in a life-or-death experiment to test the efficacy of the virus. Join Matt and his assistant Delia Perez as their investigation exposes a group of turncoat scientists willing to sell their deadly secrets to a cabal of malevolent enemies.

PART I

The white four-door coupe sat idling, parked under a large tree outside the bowling alley, the car's air-conditioner straining against the oppressive summer heat. The wraparound sunglasses and dark suit worn by the driver added an element of cloak and dagger to the scheduled meeting. The driver craned his head in the direction of the double doors just as I walked out of the main entry and in the direction of the coupe. I opened the passenger door and climbed inside.

"Thanks for meeting me here."

"No problem," I reassured the driver. Two hours and a telephone call earlier, I had agreed to meet the caller. The conversation was otherwise unremarkable with the exception of the caller's insistence we meet privately, along with a description of the vehicle and where it would be parked. "So, what's this all about?" I asked.

"One of our employees, a scientist, is missing. He disappeared five days ago during his lunch break."

I pulled a face. "Missing scientist? You didn't say anything about anyone missing when we spoke earlier."

The driver sighed nervously. "You're right, I didn't, not even my name or who I'm affiliated with," he reminded me, fidgeting with his glasses and checking his rear view and side door mirrors.

I pivoted and faced the driver. "Then start talking," I demanded, "or the meeting is over."

That was all the additional impetus needed. Wayne Hutchinson was a biotechnologist with Virolabs, Inc., located in the middle of a desolate wasteland on the outskirts of the city limits. The only thing I knew about the rectangular-shaped, drab concrete-constructed facility prior to Hutchinson's earlier call was that it was built approximately ten years ago. I nodded again. "All right, now tell me about your missing colleague."

"Harold Mitchell, fifty-eight years old, a widower," Hutchinson answered. "He's the chief virologist, a scientist responsible for the Omega Project, a research effort to create a hemorrhagic virus more contagious and deadly than anything known in nature or previously created. Plainly stated, it could threaten millions of lives."

I rubbed my chin pensively. *Damn, there's no way I could have guessed this was coming.* "And who's responsible for the order to create this virus—and why?"

"Let's just say that since they lifted the ban on making lethal viruses, the justification for the creation of these deadly pathogens is deemed necessary."

"Necessary? Necessary for what?"

"For the development of strategies and effective countermeasures against new pathogens that pose a threat to public health—the so-called 'official' rationale for the R&D necessary to produce these microorganisms," he replied.

"Who's *they*?" I insisted.

"Who do you think?" Hutchinson said with enough sarcasm that further explanation wasn't necessary.

Another nod. "Yeah, okay, I get it." *I'm no scientist, but*

I don't have to be to know that that kind of sanctioned research could unleash a new and unpredictable contagion if not properly safeguarded—or should it escape from his lab—or any lab, I thought.

"Which is *exactly* why I'm here," Hutchinson fired back, fear written all over his face.

Taking in a breath, I locked eyes with Hutchinson. "So, not only is the chief scientist missing, the hemorrhagic virus he's responsible for creating has vanished as well. Are we on the same page?"

The biotechnologist bobbed his head. "Mitchell has disappeared, along with two vials of a biosafety level 4 virus."

"Biosafety level 4?"

"That's what I said. There are four biosafety levels, BSL-1 through BSL-4, with BSL-4 being the highest level of containment. This hemorrhagic virus is a BSL-4 pathogen."

"How do you know the vials are missing?"

"I spoke with Mitchell's assistant. Her name is Joan Miller. She informed me privately that her boss and both vials are missing—then swore me to secrecy. She's shook up—and scared."

"Go on—keep talking," I prodded.

"That's all I know. Before Joan's disclosure, we thought he'd taken a few days off, then rumors began to circulate about Mitchell being AWOL. Everything from he had resigned to he's been kidnapped and is being held hostage—either by criminals, terrorists, or a rogue foreign government."

"Anything from the bio-lab director or his associates?"

"Nothing. And no one has been questioned by local or state law enforcement—or the feds. Nobody under-stands why they're being so hush. That's the catalyst for the rumors. People start coming up with their own theories and scenarios. And it makes them fearful they might be next. You can't blame them."

I nodded in agreement. "Is that why you keep checking your rear view mirrors?"

"Yes . . . I mean, what do you think?" Hutchinson answered nervously.

I let out an exasperated sigh. "What do I think?" I parroted, followed by a pause. "Well, the word *espionage* is the first thought that pops up in my head. *Terrorism* is another. And old-fashioned *criminal theft for ransom* completes the list."

Hutchinson craned his head in my direction. "That's why we contacted you. The senior project virologist and two vials of a deadly virus he created are missing, and no one is talking to us or saying a damn thing. We need some answers," the technologist pleaded.

The vehicle's air conditioner provided little relief from the sweltering heat. I turned, facing the front windshield. After adjusting the air flow on the dashboard supply vent and loosening my tie, I pivoted back in Hutchinson's direction. "All right, I'll do what I can."

Hutchinson pursed his lips in a half-smile, relieved at my answer. "What else do you need from me?" he asked.

"A bio of Mitchell, a recent photo, and his home address to start."

Hutchinson turned and reached behind the driver's side seat. He grabbed a small briefcase by the handle sitting on the rear floorboard and pulled it over, setting it awkwardly on the center console. He opened the briefcase and removed an unlabeled office file. "Here—everything you need to know about Mitchell is in the folder," he said, handing the binder to me.

There's no question the feds are involved, even if Hutchison doesn't believe so, I thought, opening the makeshift dossier. Visually scanning the documents and passport-size photo taped to the inside cover of the file, I closed the folder and looked up at Hutchinson.

"This will do for now. I'll be in touch. You spoke with my assistant Delia earlier when you called and asked for me. She's fully briefed on every case I handle. Keep that in mind when communicating with her—*capisce?*"

"Understood," Hutchinson said.

"Oh, and one more thing," I continued, opening the passenger side door and stepping out, my dress shirt soaked with perspiration.

"What's that?" Hutchinson asked, a curious expression appearing.

"Do something about your air conditioner."

PART II

"The FBI was on this two days ago," Agent Morelli disclosed.

"Yeah, I figured that," I said, my iPhone held securely in place by the phone holder on the center console. Turning onto a main thoroughfare, I was only minutes away from pulling into my agency's parking lot.

"That's all I can tell you for the moment, Matt. Why don't we meet at our favorite watering hole," he suggested. "Now that you're involved in the case, I can shed a little more light on what we believe might be happening."

"Sounds good to me. I owe you a drink anyway," I chuckled. "Give me an hour. I have a few things I need to take care of."

Parking and exiting my car, I casually walked into the office. Delia, sitting at her desk, looked up and over her laptop's screen, acknowledging my presence with a smile. She moved her hand across the keyboard, pressed the enter button, then slowly pushed the screen down and closed the computer.

"It's hot out there today," I complained, removing my sports jacket and loosening the matching tie.

"According to the internet it's going to be toasty all

week," Delia said, lightly tapping the cover of her laptop several times.

"Yeah, I get it," I muttered, standing next to my assistant's desk.

"How did the meeting go?"

I took in a deep breath, then slowly exhaled. "Hot as the weather. Why don't you come into my office; I'll bring you up to date on what we're dealing with."

Minutes later, after I wrapped up my brief with Delia, she pushed her chair away from my desk and stood. "Sounds like more than you bargained for," she cautioned.

"Before this is all over, I might wind up agreeing with you," I admitted, a wry expression appearing. "In the meantime, we're on the case, as well as our friends with the FBI. In fact, I'm on my way to meet Morelli. Use the remainder of the day to find out everything you can about our missing scientist," I directed, handing Delia the file I received from Hutchinson.

"I'm on it," she said, turning around and walking back to her desk.

* * *

"We still don't have enough information to make an assessment regarding what we're dealing with," Morelli confided. Sitting across the table from me, he took a sip of his drink, a Jack Daniels on the rocks.

"Then what *does* the FBI have? You didn't invite me over here just to tell me you've made no progress."

"No, I didn't," Morelli responded. "We combed the inside and outside of his home, along with his vehicle, which, by the way, is still parked in the garage. No evidence related to his disappearance was discovered, no vials were found, nor was his home or vehicle ransacked. We departed his house shortly thereafter, locked it up tight, and turned the lights off. We did speak with his only neighbor, a lady by the name of Susan Caine, a widow who resides in the house nearest our missing scientist. She told us she thought she heard what sounded like shouting coming from the Mitchell home around three a.m. or so."

"Was she awake, or did the shouting awaken her?"

"Neither. Mrs. Caine had retired earlier in the evening. She set the alarm on her cell phone for three a.m. to check on her cat, who two days earlier was brought home from the vet. She wanted to make sure the cat was okay through the early morning."

"Other than the noise, did she see anything?"

"She noticed a back porch light go on for about ten seconds, then off. That was it. She didn't see Mitchell or anyone else."

"So, where does that leave things?"

"That's all I can tell you for now," Morelli said.

I straightened, irritated by the hesitancy of my FBI associate and friend to provide any further information. I knew Morelli was holding back. "I'd like to talk to her," I proposed, lifting and finishing the mug of beer I was holding.

Morelli grinned. "You took the words right out of my mouth. I was going to suggest you do just that. We had an entire forensics team on Mitchell's property at the time we questioned Mrs. Caine. She seemed more rattled by our presence and questions than the disappearance of her neighbor."

I laughed. "Yeah, you were the sheriff and neighbor-hood welcome wagon all rolled into one. Did you remember to leave her with a gift basket?"

"Very funny," Morelli smirked, "which is exactly the reason why I believe she'll be more receptive to you dropping by. Mrs. Caine might be less ruffled by your presence than a throng of FBI agents swarming all over her property. She may have remembered something after we left—or decide to reveal something she knows and didn't want to share with us." Morelli leaned forward. "You might even uncover something new, although you didn't hear me say that."

I nodded. I understood the innuendo. "I'll bring Delia with me. She might feel more comfortable in the presence of another female."

"Good idea," Morelli proclaimed. He finished his drink then stood. "Good to see you again, Matt. I'll be in touch."

"Later, Frank."

Morelli turned and walked toward the exit.

It was a little after seven p.m. I thought about ordering another beer, then changed my mind. I stood, threw a five spot on the table, and walked out of the pub. As I drove back to my office, my thoughts focused on dropping by the Caine residence the following day, unannounced, with Delia accompanying me. Just before I reached the agency's parking lot, I made a quick U-turn. *Delia's gone home for the day—probably wouldn't hurt to complete a quick drive-by. At least I'll know where I'm going tomorrow.*

For half an hour I followed the directions voiced by the GPS app on my iPhone. "It's remote, but close to the lab," I mumbled. The home's address did appear to correlate somewhat with the location of the bio-tech lab where the missing scientist was employed. A thick forest of trees lined the two-lane winding roads leading to the unincorporated area of the county. The locale encompassed only a handful of isolated homes. *If you like privacy, this is probably as good a place as any.*

Navigating my way around several winding roads, I finally turned onto a narrow side street leading to the scientist's residence. I pushed the passenger side down window switch and removed my foot off the pedal to allow my car to idle slowly up the road. Approximately an eighth of a mile into my search for Mitchell's home, I happened upon a house to my right, set back quite a distance from the shoulder, a numbered postbox attached to the top of a four-by-four mailbox post that looked more like a birdhouse than an actual mailbox. The number on the box corresponded with the information Morelli provided earlier.

I tapped the brakes, then stared for several moments at the log-cabin-style home. It was the Caine residence. Soft illumination from inside the home confirmed the house was occupied.

Taking my foot off the brake, I continued up the tree-lined road for a short distance until reaching a stop sign. Turning left per the GPS, I continued another eighth of a mile until noticing an oversized, premium streetside metal mailbox supported by a metal four-by-four. Three-inch reflective house numbers were plainly visible on the box. *Here we are*, I thought. I tapped the brakes again. Unlike the Caine residence, the Mitchell home was more traditional country in its architectural design, but with one notable difference: Lights, although dim, were clearly visible on the inside.

"Somebody's there," I whispered.

PART III

Killing the engine and lights, I stepped out of my vehicle. I took a quick look around, allowing the driver's-side door to rest gently against the door frame. It was a moonless night and dark as ten feet down in every direction, the dim light emanating from inside the front of the Mitchell home the only exception. Using the light as a beacon, I walked ahead of my car, finally spotting an asphalt driveway that ultimately curved in the direction of an attached side-entry two-car garage.

Following the driveway, I quickly made my way to the front of the garage door. At the rear of the house, I climbed a short stairway leading to a redwood deck attached to the back of the Mitchell home. I scooted quietly around the usual complement of patio furniture until my back was flat against the wood-framed structure, just on the edge of the sliding glass door on the back of the house. Vertical blinds on the opposite side of the sliding glass doors appeared disheveled, as if they had been roughly pushed aside. Upon closer inspection, I noticed the sliding door was slightly ajar. *Just enough for someone to have squeezed through.*

Removing my snub-nosed revolver from its holster, I carefully edged my way inside, working my way toward what appeared to be the kitchen, its shape and layout made visible by the dim light filtering its way around the corner of a dividing wall. Continuing toward an archway, I leaned forward just enough to see around its edge, a small lamp with a low-wattage bulb on top of an upright piano, the culprit responsible for the vague lighting. *The living room, the front of the home . . . Okay, so why is it on?*

"Hands up—don't move," a muffled voice ordered. I felt the hard metal of a gun barrel connect with the middle of my back. The unidentified male grabbed my short-barreled revolver with his other hand, snatching it roughly away. Following me after a shove through the archway, the perp blurted out, "Who are you—what are you doing here?"

"Funny, I was just about to ask you the same question," I replied in a cynical tone, turning my head toward the voice.

"Don't look at me—and don't turn around," the guy barked. "Hand me your wallet, the one with your ID and badge in it—and be slow about it."

I removed the bifold ID out of the left inside pocket of my sports jacket with my right hand then extended my arm to the unknown party behind me. Just as he reached for it, I allowed the wallet to slip out of my hand. The perp focused on the wallet as it dropped to the floor. One moment of distraction was all I needed. In an instant I wheeled around, knocking the gun out the thug's gloved hand with my left arm, simultaneously connecting with a right hook to the left side of his jaw.

Charging out of a bedroom hallway, another unknown party crashed into me like a runaway freight train, slamming both of us to the floor. A brief struggle ensued. I managed to stand, yanking the second perp to his feet before smashing him in the face with a right cross, dropping the assailant like a ton of bricks.

Taking a deep breath and attempting to get my

bearings, I took a step back. That's when I felt the thud of metal on the back of my head.

* * *

"He's coming around," said a barely audible voice I recognized.

"Matt, it's me, Delia," she repeated several times, kneeling next to me on the floor. She had placed several folded kitchen towels under my head as she gently wiped my face and forehead with a damp cloth.

"It could have been worse," another familiar voice blurted. "What the hell was he doing here at this time of night? And by himself, for crying out loud."

I strained to sit up, holding the back of my head with my hand. I squinted in response to most of the lights inside the Mitchell home being turned on. Tilting my head back slightly, I looked up at Delia and Agent Morelli standing next to her. "Don't tell me . . . the GPS button?"

"You're fortunate Delia was up at two o'clock this morning, checking on your whereabouts," Morelli barked. Behind him, several other agents and technicians were searching the house again for evidence.

"What are you talking about?" I fired back.

"He means I was at the office at seven p.m. waiting for you," Delia answered. "When you didn't return by nine, I left and went home. I started tracking your whereabouts. When the GPS indicated you were still at the same location at two a.m., I called Frank."

Matt stood, helped to his feet by Delia and Morelli. "I just wanted to get a heads-up on the exact location of Mitchell's home, as well as his neighbor, Susan Caine." I grimaced, holding the back of my head before pivoting unsteadily, facing Morelli. "I noticed a light on in the Mitchell home, and . . ."

"And you just had to check it out—by yourself," Morelli interrupted, noticeable irritation in his voice.

"How did I know anyone was inside—none of them Harold Mitchell?" I scoffed.

A crime scene technician walked up to Morelli. "Nothing of any evidentiary value has been discovered. A few cabinets and drawers have been rifled through, but that's about it. We haven't dusted for prints."

"You won't find any—those guys were gloved."

"Do it anyway," Morelli ordered.

I let out a deep breath. "Like I said earlier, Frank, I wanted to get a heads-up on both addresses. My first thought when I noticed the light was on was that it was Mitchell—that he was home."

"Uh, hmm," Morelli grumbled. "So, how did that work out for you?" he asked, still irritated as he looked around the disheveled room.

"Delia and I will return tomorrow and speak with Mrs. Caine," I said, purposefully ignoring his question.

"I'm afraid that won't be necessary," Morelli responded.

"What do you mean it won't be necessary?"

Delia turned and faced me. "She's dead."

PART IV

"Murdered," Morelli explained. "We found her in the master bedroom. She was lying face-up on top of her California king; dried blood on her face and pillow, bruising around the nose and mouth, and bloodshot eyes appear to indicate death by smothering. My agents and evidence techs are still investigating. The body has been removed by the coroner."

"When was she discovered?"

"Within minutes after we found you unconscious on the floor, around three in the morning, after which I remembered noticing her lights were still on as we drove to this location. That struck me as odd, so I sent our people back to her home. There was no forcible entry, so I'm guessing she must have known the people involved."

I shook my head. I looked around the room, noticing the overturned furniture and chairs. "With the exception of Mrs. Caine, this just gets better with every passing day," I declared, a note of sarcasm in my voice.

"You should have that goose egg on your head checked out," Morelli suggested. "You still look a little woozy. Call it a night, Duggan. Let Delia drive you to the ER; have them take a look at you."

"What about Mrs. Caine?"

"My people are still there. We'll wrap things up with her. I'll follow up with you tomorrow and fill you in," Morelli assured me.

* * *

"I thought we were going to the hospital," Delia protested, but I directed her to drive to the office instead.

"That's exactly what I want Morelli to think we're doing. Did you find out anything on our missing scientist after I left the office earlier to meet our FBI friend?"

"I did—and you're not going to believe what I discovered."

"Did you share any of it with—"

"No, I didn't," Delia interrupted. "Although I was so upset when we arrived at Mitchell's home, I was tempted to. Add to that Mrs. Caine's murder."

"Yeah, somebody wanted her quiet," I mumbled, rubbing my chin.

"My point is they could have killed you as well," Delia said. She craned her head in my direction. "Are you sure you don't want to go to the hospital and get checked out? How do you know you don't have a concussion?"

"I'm all right," I mumbled, placing a reassuring hand on her forearm. "We'll stop at a drive-through and order a quick breakfast. Then we'll return to the office and go over what you've uncovered. And let's do a background check and history on Mrs. Caine while we're at it. People aren't usually whacked for no reason."

Nodding and watching the road, Delia exhaled a resigned sigh.

* * *

Arriving back at the agency, Delia followed me into the reception area. I opened my office door and walked inside; no sooner had I turned on the light, the chair behind my desk quickly swung around, occupied by a man wearing a ski mask and holding a gun. Dressed in a dark suit and tie and wearing gloves, he pointed the revolver directly at me. "Don't try anything stupid," he ordered, standing and pushing the chair away.

I immediately recognized the perp's tone. *Same voice I heard at Mitchell's home.*

"Get inside," another unidentified gruff voice shouted. Delia was roughly pushed into my office by a second identically dressed and masked male.

"What's this all about?"

"You'll find out soon enough," the first perp sneered. Glancing at his accomplice, he barked, "Get his gun—and his cell phone."

The second thug zip-tied me, followed by Delia. He removed a pair of hoods out of his jacket, throwing them over our heads.

"Let's go," the first culprit barked. As they guided us both out of the office and toward a waiting vehicle outside, I estimated the time at approximately four thirty a.m. I knew activity outside the agency would be minimal, making it less likely someone would notice and call the police. Delia and I would have to play it by ear for the time being.

We were shoved into the backseat of a car, then the rear doors slammed shut, followed by the driver's side and front passenger's-side doors. The sound of tires screeching served to confirm completion of the planned abduction.

"Where are you taking us?" I shouted, my voice muffled by the hood.

"It doesn't matter—we've got the both of you," the

second henchman snickered. "Shut up and don't give us any trouble."

* * *

Approximately an hour and several short turns later, the vehicle came to a stop. Delia and I were removed from the back seat and guided up a short stairwell and through the door of a dwelling. We were seated in what felt like standard office chairs.

"Take off their coverings," another unfamiliar voice ordered.

Removing the hoods, we squinted against the brightness of the lighted room, attempting to adjust our focus on the man now sitting before us. My wrists burned from the tightness of the zip ties.

"Why were we brought here?" I growled, my vision sharpening to full clarity. Staring intently into the face of the man sitting behind a desk, my expression immediately contorted to one of total surprise. "Wait a minute," I gasped. "You're Harold Mitchell, the missing scientist." I tried to make sense of what was happening while looking around the room. "What the hell is going on?"

Stone-faced, Mitchell stood. He walked from behind the desk, then next to the chairs that seated Delia and me. "Unfortunately, neither you nor your colleague will live long enough to find out." He continued to pace the room. "You asked why you and your colleague were brought here," the now-discovered scientist continued. "Very simple," he answered. "Remember the old cliché, curiosity killed the cat?"

I pursed my lips and shook my head. "Quit playing games and get to the point," I demanded.

Shrugging indifferently, Mitchell leaned forward, locking eyes with his tethered captives. "As . . . you . . . wish . . ." he jeered. "You and Ms. Perez have volunteered to participate in my own mini-clinical trial to test the effects of my newest lab-created virus, appropriately named systemic hemorrhagic virus."

Delia turned her head in my direction. "What the hell is he talking about?"

"He's telling us, in his own perverted way, that we got a little too nosey, and now we're going to pay the price."

"Took the words right out of my mouth," Mitchell jumped in. "The dangers involved with too much investigation—as suggested by the previous idiom," he clarified.

"And you actually believe enrolling us in your warped science project is going to prove anything?" I sneered.

A devilish grin flickered across Mitchell's face. "We'll soon find out." He nodded. "Take them to the basement," he shouted at his henchman.

PART V

"Matt's not answering—neither is Delia," Morelli grumbled, throwing his landline receiver at its cradle. His partner stood in front of the lead agent's desk.

"It's unlikely calls to both would go unanswered," Agent Anderson surmised. "Should we pay your friends a visit?"

Taking a breath, Morelli pushed his chair away from his desk and stood. "Let's go," he bellowed.

* * *

Escorted downstairs and into the basement, Delia and I quickly realized the sectional cellar had been converted into a makeshift lab. It was a dim, blue fluorescent-lit area, illuminated that way during inactivity. A variety of lab equipment was stacked and arranged neatly on multiple benches. Almost everything was white—the floor, ceiling, walls, tables, and drawers. On top of a small desk, a computer hummed away, its display screen blank. The smell alternated between a sickening aroma of days-old chicken broth and diluted Gatorade, the result of work Mitchell was involved with.

Turning on the main basement fluorescent lights, we

were guided to the end of the lab and toward a second section of the basement encompassing an empty room. The steel walls were a light green. The room's egress was via a heavy, hermetically sealed stainless steel sliding door, designed to be opened and closed by use of a large handle to slide the door left and right on its track. The door was manufactured with a sealed viewing window, appearing to be twelve inches square centered approximately eighteen inches from the top. Four small fluorescent ceiling lights illuminated the inside, highlighting its eerie green coloring. The room was large enough to accommodate several folding chairs and two cots.

One of Mitchell's minions unlocked the door and slid it to the left. "Both of you—inside," he ordered.

Hesitating, I stepped into the chamber, followed by Delia. To say I was apprehensive was an understatement. Working together for many years on a multitude of cases would on occasion result in one or both of us engaged in dangerous, even life-threatening situations, but never one in which we would soon find ourselves the subject of biological experimentation. I was worried—not for myself, but for Delia.

Turning around and staring at Mitchell's minion, I shouted, "Okay, so what's—"

Wham! Before I even finished my question, the criminal thug had slid the door shut, locking automatically. Like a police cruiser, there was no door handle or locking mechanism on the inside. The perp banged on the thick glass viewing window, waving and smiling like a sadistic fiend before turning off the main fluorescent white lights and walking away. Through the door window the basement resumed its dim, but eerie soft blue lighting.

"May as well have a seat," Delia said, using her foot

to pull a chair away from a wall. Craning her head in my direction, she sighed. "I almost hate saying and asking, but, just out of *curiosity,* what was your question, before Mr. Manners closed the door in your face?"

Still staring at the door, I pivoted. "Uh . . . next . . . what's next?" I mumbled, turning around and walking toward the second chair.

Delia chuckled nervously. "I don't think either of us wants to know what's *next.*"

Her utterance prompted me to think back to my childhood. My parents were devout Catholics, which meant strict adherence to weekly Mass. I was nine when my mother passed away after a long illness, leaving just my father and me. He frequently reminded me that going to church was non-negotiable. "I made a promise to your mother that I would take you to Mass," he would often say. I never particularly cared for the weekly Eucharist as insisted on by my father, but as I grew older, something changed. I took comfort in dropping by the church on occasion, particularly when the chapel was empty of parishioners. Private medi-tation brought me a great deal of comfort, especially during and after a time of crisis or uncertainty. I did that after my detective partner and friend Seth was killed, and I instinc-tively found myself yearning for it again.

"I *will* say this," I muttered, my thoughts reverting back to the present as I continued to look around the room. "This chamber of horrors is everything a missing scientist might need—even one that has apparently gone rogue—perhaps even insane."

* * *

"Neither one is here," Agent Anderson informed Morelli, walking out of Matt's office. Ross and Davidson, two other agents, having checked out the upstairs, reported no physical evidence to indicate any kind of a scuffle or altercation had occurred. "Other than their absence, everything appears to be in order," Anderson added.

"Everything except the front door is unlocked, the office lights are off, it's ten a.m., and both are missing," Morelli continued.

"Frank, they're not answering their landline at home or their cell phone," Agent Davidson reported, "but I did find a purse with an iPhone in it in Delia's desk drawer." He handed the phone to Morelli. "It's off."

He powered up the phone and the passcode screen appeared. "It could be hers," he guessed. "Either her primary or back up phone. She's a sharp-witted investigator. What Matt lacks, she complements."

Returning Davidson's glance, Morelli bellowed, "I want you and Ross to drive to their homes—see if either or both are there." Turning to Anderson and gently wobbling the iPhone, he added, "Let's take this cell phone back to the forensics lab and see if they can crack this passcode without losing any data. If my hunch is correct, we may have just located both."

* * *

"Insane? Now I *am* freaking out," Delia shouted.

I wheeled in her direction, a concerned expression showing. "You've always insisted on transparency, even during our most dangerous cases. Talk to me, Delia. Am I missing something here?"

She fidgeted in her seat. "Remember when you asked

if I uncovered anything regarding our missing scientist?"

I looked up at the ceiling, then down again. "Mhm, yeah, I remember. You told me I wouldn't believe what you uncovered."

Delia sighed. "Talk about coincidence—but before I tell you, do you think it's time we free ourselves from these zip cuffs?"

I grinned. "It's our ticket out of here. Do you still remember how?"

Chuckling, Delia stood. "Watch me," she said. Standing and moving away from her chair, she turned around so I could see the zip tie.

"I need to position the locking bar so that it's centered between your wrists, then tighten it as much as I can." I turned around; with limited use of bound hands, I managed to do both. Delia's face contorted with pain, the plasticuffs cutting into her wrists like a searing hot wire.

"Okay, give it a try," I said.

Stooping down several inches, Delia leaned forward. She raised her arms behind her back as high as she could. In one swift motion she slammed her arms down, her wrists making contact with her pelvic bone. Nothing. She tried again, still nothing.

"You can do it, Delia."

Pursing her lips and grimacing with pain, she tried a third time. The zip tie snapped.

"Good job."

Massaging her bloodied wrists for a few moments, she walked behind me. Using a manicured fingernail to create a gap in the locking bar on my zip tie, she pulled the strap backward until it was all the way out. I kicked both under the closest cot.

"Okay," I told her while rubbing my wrists, "when

those bozos return, I want you on the floor—with your hands behind your back. I'll concoct some phony story you fainted, then hit your head when you fell. I doubt Mitchell will want to test his virus on any of his captives who are unconscious or injured. That should get him or his goons to open the door."

Delia held up her hands. "My wrists are bleeding."

"Sorry. Looks like I pulled your zip tie too tight."

Delia smiled. "It'll make your story more convincing that I hit my head. I can pool some of the blood on the floor, smear a little on my forehead and side of my face, then position myself with my head next to a pool of blood."

I grinned again. "Now you know why I hired you," I said, patting her on the shoulder.

"Unlike the walls, the floor is white," Delia pointed out. "It should be easy for them to see the blood on the floor through the door window."

I pondered. "We have to time this just right. We don't know exactly when they'll be back."

Delia smeared blood on the floor. Using my pocket square as a paint brush, I dabbed my handkerchief on her bloodied wrists, covering the right side of her forehead and temporal area down to the front of her ear. She sat on the floor, ready to lie face-up with her hands behind her back. I stood next to the door window. We waited.

PART VI

The soft glow of the white fluorescent lights filtered through the small window of the hermetically sealed door. I turned and glanced at Delia.

"Are they on their way?" she whispered.

"Yeah, they are," I whispered back. "Go ahead and position yourself on the floor."

Satisfied Delia's theatrics were sufficiently realistic, I clasped my hands together behind my back. I pressed my front torso against the door, my face adjacent to the viewing window.

Noticing Delia on the floor through the door's window, the alpha thug turned his head around. "Something's wrong with the girl," he told Mitchell behind him. "She's on the floor. There's blood on her face."

"Move," Mitchell ordered. Let me have a look."

I pounded on the steel door with my knee. "She needs help," I yelled.

"What happened?" Mitchell asked, peering through the viewing window.

"She fainted, then fell and hit her head on the floor. I haven't been able to revive her. She has a gash on her forehead and she's bleeding out of her ear."

The rogue scientist understood enough to know that

clear fluids or blood emanating from the nose or ears of an injured party was a distinct sign of a serious head injury. Stepping back, he motioned for his main henchman to unlock the door.

"Step away from the door, Duggan," the primary thug snarled, gun in hand.

My hands clasped behind me, I backed away several steps, careful not to reveal my wrists were no longer bound. The door handle engaged on the opposite side with a distinctive *thunk*, followed by the door sliding to the left on its track. The perp's accomplice entered first, followed by Mitchell's primary enforcer. Standing next to Delia, the alpha thug's associate turned his head around. "Hey boss, do you want—"

Delia grabbed both hems of the kidnapper's utility pants, yanking his feet out from underneath him. Pulled completely off both feet, he fell backward with such force his head reverberated with the sound of a sickening *crack* against the concrete floor. It was lights out.

Startled by the suddenness of Delia's movement, the primary perp glanced in the direction of his partner. That's all the diversion I needed. In an instant I stepped forward, delivering a power punch to the jaw of Mitchell's chief minion. He dropped like a lead balloon, falling to the floor next to his partner-in-crime. I lurched out of the room, sprinting for Mitchell, now running for the stairwell leading to the first floor of the unfamiliar dwelling.

He had just placed a foot on the first step when I grabbed him and jerked his right arm up behind his back. "Aargh," Mitchell groaned. "What are you doing?"

"It's called a hammerlock. Let me know if this tickles," I snarled, ratcheting his arm further with a burning twist.

"You and I are walking back to your makeshift Tower of London. *Move*, mister."

"Aargh," Mitchell cried out louder. "Okay, okay, whatever you say."

Grasping the shoulder of the rogue scientist's white lab coat with my left hand, I directed Mitchell back to the same creepy room where Delia and I were held captive just moments earlier. She was standing outside the chamber, the door closed and locked.

"I have your gun and both their guns," Delia said.

"Good. How are the two goons?"

"Sound asleep, with their hands triple zip-tied behind them," she added with a smile, twirling an unused tie in front of Mitchell. "Their jackets were stuffed with these things, along with what appears to be a key to the door upstairs."

"What is your plan for me?" Mitchell asked nervously.

"In a moment you'll be joining your two sidekicks inside your own mini-gas chamber while we contact the FBI. But first, you're going to tell me where those missing vials are."

Silence.

I torqued Mitchell's right arm. He screamed.

"I'll twist your sorry-ass arm right off."

"All right, all right," Mitchell cried out.

I loosened my grip. "And I'm not going to ask you again—where are they?"

Mitchell gasped, attempting to catch his breath and re-orient himself as the pain in his arm lessened. "They're in the lab," he confessed. "The vials are in cryopreserved freezers in a separate room underneath the stairwell."

"Have you opened the vials since bringing them here?"

"No," Mitchell said. "This lab is only equipped to

handle BSL-1 pathogens."

"You mean until *we* were abducted," Delia angrily retorted. "I know the difference between biosafety levels regarding pathogens, and those vials you removed from Virolabs contain a BSL-4 microorganism. You were only hours, perhaps minutes away from ramping it up to BSL-4 with Matt and me as the guinea pigs."

"That explains the hermetically sealed chamber," I jumped in, checking out the door again from the outside, and quickly glancing into the room through the viewing window. Mitchell's thugs remained motionless on the concrete floor.

"Listen, I—"

"What were you planning to do with that virus after your mad scientist experiment with us was over?" I interrupted.

Mitchell clammed up.

"Yeah, that's what I thought," I responded in frustration, exchanging glances with Delia. "When Frank and his prosecutor friends explain the decades he's facing in prison, he may be a little more cooperative."

Delia pivoted toward the scientist. "Turn around," she snapped.

Complying, Mitchell slowly completed an about-face. She secured Mitchell's wrists with three zip ties, tightening each one with a firm yank, a sharp hissing sound audible with each tug.

"Do you have to tighten them like that?" Mitchell asked, cringing with pain.

"How do *you* like it?" Delia taunted.

Matt grabbed the door handle and pulled, unlocking the chamber's portal and sliding it to the left. I shot an unsympathetic gaze at Mitchell. "Step inside.

PART VII

Handing the iPhone back to Morelli, the forensic lab specialist informed the lead FBI agent the cell phone was unlocked. "Here you go," he said. "The data appears to be intact, including the GPS app."

"Thanks," Morelli mumbled, looking at the screen on Delia's phone. "This is exactly what I was looking for." He tapped and reviewed the GPS app knowing it was linked to Matt's tracking button, then glanced at Agent Anderson. "Make arrangements for a helicopter."

"I'm on it," Anderson replied.

* * *

I watched through the viewing window as Mitchell, locked in the chamber with his two unconscious minions, took a seat on the edge of a cot. The rogue scientist looked around the room, a befuddled expression etched all over his face.

I turned in Delia's direction and chuckled. "You should see the look on Mitchell's kisser—a Kodak moment for sure."

Delia smirked. "He can't believe he's locked up in his own jail."

"Let's go upstairs and figure out where we are."

"Should we confirm the vials are in those freezers?" Delia asked.

"Too risky," I said. "Better let the people at Virolabs do that wearing the appropriate bio-level suits. If there's been any leakage or spillage, and we open those . . ."

"Yeah, I get it," Delia acknowledged.

* * *

"Still no answer," Morelli yelled out loud into his headset, turning his head and glancing at Anderson in the chopper's backseat, the roar of the helicopter's engine near deafening. Shaking his head in frustration, he returned his personal cell phone to the inside pocket of his suit jacket. He glanced again at Delia's iPhone secured inside a cell phone holder mounted on the helo's dashboard. "If Matt and Delia have been abducted, as I suspect, the perpetrators have either destroyed or discarded his cell phone."

"Agents Ross and Davidson are tailing us now," Anderson said, leaning forward and tapping Morelli on the shoulder. "They're following the helo's GPS. I just received their text."

"Tell them to adjust their radio frequency to the chopper's transceiver. We'll keep following Delia's GPS."

"About fifteen minutes," the pilot shouted.

* * *

"There's nothing in Mitchell's desk with an address on it," Delia muttered in an irritated tone, rifling through his desk drawers. "But here's a key fob with two keys attached."

"It might belong to the vehicle we were brought here

in. Let's check outside."

A late model four-door sedan sat parked in the middle of a semi-circular driveway. The raised brick stairway led to a wraparound cedar porch enveloping the entire dwelling. The porch offered a panoramic view of the immediate area. The large two-story estate was isolated. Sporadic tufts of trees, and on-again, off-again grasses and shrubs as far as the eye could see topped the brown earthen crust, a surface that looked as hard as stone and somehow even less inviting.

"It's a Cadillac CT6," I yelled out, pressing the fob button and hearing the doors unlock.

"I don't care if it's a Depression-era tractor with three square wheels," Delia declared. "C'mon Matt, this house of horrors is creeping me out," she pleaded.

I laughed. "All right, let's go."

Delia recalled our time of arrival to Mitchell's dungeon was approximately an hour following our abduction. "An hour's drive would be about forty to sixty miles considering route, speed, traffic conditions, and so on. Unless they were driving in circles, we crossed several county lines, so we'll stop at the first convenience store or other business we come across and contact Morelli."

"Fine with me," Delia replied. "Make it a convenience store, I'm starving."

* * *

"That's where the GPS is leading us," the pilot observed, pointing a finger at an isolated dwelling approximately two miles ahead.

Morelli noticed a clump of trees a hundred yards in front of the building. "Set us down behind those trees," he told the pilot.

Rotors spinning and guns drawn, Morelli and his partner exited the chopper and approached the front door of the isolated dwelling. Standing on either side of the doorway, Morelli banged hard on the center panel. "This is the FBI—open up."

No response.

He pounded the door again with the side of his closed fist. "FBI," he yelled a second time. "Answer the door."

Again, no reaction or reply.

He grabbed the doorknob and gave it a turn. To his surprise it was unlocked. Giving a gentle push, Morelli and his colleague stared cautiously at the partially exposed inside of the main floor of the dwelling. Stepping inside, they spent the first several minutes moving from room to room.

"This floor is clear, Frank. There's no upstairs, but the room beyond that doorway appears to be an office." Morelli and Anderson walked up to a desk on the opposite side.

Catching something out of the corner of his eye, Morelli reached down and picked up a small, coin-shaped white object sitting on the edge of the desk. "Well, I'll be damned," he muttered, rendering a fiery stare at the tracking button.

"What is it, Frank?" Anderson asked.

"This is what we've been chasing," he said, showing the button to Anderson and holding it next to Delia's cell phone. Morelli tapped the GPS app on Delia's iPhone, shutting it down.

"They were obviously brought here," Anderson said.

"This place is too large not to have another floor. Let's look for a basement access," Morelli suggested.

"Bingo," Anderson yelled, noticing what appeared to be a concealed panel. "There's a stairway leading to a room below the main floor."

After sliding the panel open, they tiptoed down the dimly lit fluorescent-blue stairway, semi-automatic pistols at the ready. On the basement floor, Morelli signaled his partner to check the area to his right while he turned left and walked in the opposite direction. Satisfied there was no one in the area he checked, Anderson turned around and walked in the direction of his partner. "Clear on this side," he whispered.

Standing in front of the sealed chamber and craning his neck away from the viewing window and toward Anderson, Morelli said, "You're not going to believe this."

* * *

"All right, time to call Morelli," I told Delia, borrowing the convenience store manager's cell phone and stepping outside.

"Morelli here," he answered.

"Frank—it's Matt."

"Matt! Where the devil are you?" he hollered. "Is Delia with you?"

"We're okay," I reassured Morelli. "Now, let me guess—you're at an undisclosed dwelling in a remote area that Delia and I escaped from about an hour ago; you tracked Delia's GPS button I purposely left just before we fled in their vehicle. By the way, you'll find Mitchell and his two henchmen locked up in their own test chamber down in the basement, along with the two vials he stole from Virolabs."

"You're damn lucky I found Delia's iPhone in a purse in her desk at your office," Morelli retorted.

"A moot issue, Frank. We escaped."

"Don't be a smartass, Duggan. I'm talking about had

you *not* escaped," he fired back.

I pursed my lips and nodded. Morelli was right. It was sheer luck Delia and I were able to turn the tables on Mitchell and his two thugs, and flee.

"You and Delia need to get back here," Morelli demanded.

"That's *your* crime scene now, Frank. We're on our way to Virolabs to make arrangements for a Bio-4 hazard team to remove the vials that are locked-up in cryo-freezers underneath the lab stairwell. That's where they are. Delia and I can lead them directly there."

"Correction—that's where they *were*," Morelli retorted.

A pause. "What are you talking about? I almost broke Mitchell's arm getting him to tell me where those vials are located. You don't believe me? Ask him."

"Can't do that," Morelli grumbled. "Mitchell and his two cohorts—they're dead."

PART VIII

"Executed," Morelli revealed. "All three shot in the back of the head."

"And the vials?" I asked, having returned to the crime scene per Morelli's request. The CSI personnel were scurrying around taking photographs, collecting trace materials and documenting the scene, swabbing areas of likely contact, attempting to collect low-level DNA and other biological evidence.

"Nothing Anderson and I observed," Morelli replied. "The missing vials are *still* missing, Duggan. If they were in the cryo-refrigerators as you stated earlier, that's no longer the case."

"What's the initial findings on the killing of Mitchell and his two henchmen?"

"Either a revolver was used, or the semi-auto shell casings were gathered before the executioner and accomplice departed."

"Or accomplices," Delia added.

Morelli gazed at Delia and nodded. "I wouldn't disagree." He turned and looked at me. "Let me see your revolver, Duggan."

"What?" I retorted, glancing at Morelli, a serious look on his face.

"You heard me—let me have your revolver."

Delia rendered an incredulous stare at the lead FBI agent. "Are you for real?"

"It's all right," I reassured Delia. I removed my .38-caliber Charter Arms snub-nose revolver from its holster, handing it to the lead FBI agent.

Morelli pushed the release button, allowing the cylinder to pop open. He turned the revolver upward; five jacketed .38-caliber rounds dropped into his gloved hand. The bullets were intact. Morelli sniffed the gun for the pungent odor of cordite, then checked the barrel for traces of carbon. He noted the gun's six-digit serial number stamped on the frame above the trigger, then handed it back to me.

"If the forensic pathologist determines the slugs are .38 caliber, we'll need to see your revolver again," Morelli said.

I smirked. "Not a problem, Frank, but I'm sure you know a .357 magnum can also fire .38-caliber rounds," I reminded the detective.

"Don't get cocky with me, Duggan. Here, take your ammo," Morelli barked, handing the five bullets back to me. Reaching into his jacket pocket, he removed Delia's cell phone and tracking button, handing both back to her. "You might want to stick this button back into your boss's clothing somewhere. It seems he has a tendency to get lost."

"Very funny, Frank. We're all laughing,"

Ignoring my comment, Morelli exchanged glances with Delia. "I'll have one of the CSI people take you both back to the agency," he told her.

* * *

"We're at a dead end," I voiced my frustration to Delia, standing adjacent to the kitchen counter in my office and pouring a cup of coffee. I offered it to her.

"No thanks," she said, shaking her head. "Now tell me something—what do you mean, we're at a . . . dead-end?"

I took a sip of my coffee. "I was confident we'd put all the pieces together after Mitchell and his two thugs were in FBI custody, considering what he had to lose in terms of a lengthy prison sentence."

"And?" Delia prodded.

"All the key players we're aware of are now dead."

Delia gently removed the coffee cup out of my hand. Placing it on the kitchen counter, she turned and gazed deeply into my overflowing brown eyes. "Remember when you returned to the office after your initial meeting with Wayne Hutchinson of Virolabs?"

I pondered for a moment. "Yes, I remember."

"You handed me a file given to you by Hutchinson. It was Mitchell's bio file."

"That's correct," I told her. "I asked you to use the remainder of the day to find out everything you could about the missing scientist."

"And I did just that," Delia replied. "My initial research confirmed there was nothing unremarkable or out of the ordinary regarding Mr. Mitchell—nothing I needed to bring to your attention."

"Okay, there were no red flags. So, why do I get the feeling you're going somewhere else with this?"

"Because I am," Delia asserted.

I nodded, then leaned against the kitchen counter. "All right, I'm listening," I said, grabbing my cup of coffee and taking a large gulp.

Delia turned and began walking slowly around the kitchen. "Mitchell's file contained a reference to his assistant, Joan Miller."

"Why wouldn't it? She was his assistant."

"The reference was in regard to a top-secret security clearance requested by Mitchell on behalf of Ms. Miller and obtained by Virolabs, Inc.," Delia explained.

"That wouldn't be unusual or out of the ordinary for an employee in her position," I suggested.

"Correct," Delia said. "And that's my point. She was working directly with Mitchell. When you briefed me after your meeting with Hutchinson, you mentioned his conversation with Joan Miller. After I noticed the reference in the file about the security clearance, I decided to run a database investigation on her as well."

"Okay, and what did your investigation reveal?"

"That her real name isn't Joan Miller. It's Joelle Lohmiller, her naturalized name, born in Dresden in the former East Germany in 1977. She emigrated to the United States in 1991 following the collapse of East Germany in 1989. She legally changed her name to Joan Miller more than ten years ago."

I washed my empty coffee cup in the sink before returning it to the dish rack. "A lot of people have emigrated to the United States from the former East Germany—that's not so unusual."

"Oh, is that so?" she replied with a smirk. "And how many worked for the former Leipzig-based research office for chemical toxicology?"

I turned off the faucet and stared momentarily at the backsplash, then quickly turned around. "Say again?"

"Uh-hum. I see I have your attention now, detective," Delia grinned. "It's—or more correctly, *was*—an East German research facility that manufactured chemical and biological weapons during its heyday in the German Democratic Republic."

Taking a deep breath and pursing my lips, I felt my frustration quickly evaporate. "I'll grab my spare cell phone and car keys."

"Are we going somewhere?" Delia knowingly asked.

"We are—back to Virolabs. Time to pay Ms. Miller—or *Ms. Lohmiller*—an unannounced visit."

PART IX

"Joan didn't come in today," Hutchinson explained.

Sitting next to Delia in front of Wayne Hutchinson's desk, I exchanged a dubious stare with the Virolab technologist. "Do you know where she resides?"

"I can pull up her address. We all have access to that information in the company's database." Hutchinson paused. "My question is—why? What's going on?"

"Mitchell is dead, that's what's going on."

Hutchinson rendered an incredulous stare. "What? What do you mean, he's . . . dead?"

Delia placed her hand on my forearm. "Apparently the FBI hasn't notified Virolabs subsequent to our leaving the crime scene."

"And Morelli isn't going to be happy when he finds out we beat him to it," I added. I locked eyes with Hutchinson. "Get her address, Wayne—we need you to come with us."

"I don't understand," he pleaded. "What's Joan got to do with this?"

"We'll explain on the way," Delia answered.

Exiting the building and departing in my vehicle, I followed the GPS instructions on Delia's cell phone. Time of arrival was estimated to be approximately twenty minutes.

Delia and I briefed Hutchinson while driving toward Miller's home.

"This is all just . . . surreal," Hutchinson sighed. "Mitchell's disappearance, now his murder, the missing vials, the secret laboratory, the FBI . . . You really believe Joan might be involved in this?" he asked.

"That's what Delia and I plan to find out," I answered.

"She's not married," Hutchinson revealed. "Other than that, I don't know anything more about her personally. On a professional level, Mitchell and Joan appeared to work well together. If there was a problem of any kind, I wasn't aware of it."

"Keep following the lady's voice—we're almost there," Delia said, alternately looking at her cell phone and each approaching street sign.

"You have arrived at your destination," the GPS announced.

Joan's residence was at the end of a cul-de-sac set between two adjacent homes spaced widely apart in a middle-to-upper-class neighborhood. All were nicely maintained, lawns and landscaping neatly trimmed. I parked my vehicle next to the concrete curb in front of the house, noting the lengthy and semi-curved driveway snaking its way to a side garage before splitting toward the front of the dwelling.

I walked toward the front door, followed by Delia and Hutchinson. Pressing the doorbell, I turned and exchanged a smile with Delia, Hutchinson staring off to the side.

Opening the door the length of the attached security chain, an attractive, middle-age woman with shoulder-length sandy blonde hair pressed her face close to the narrow opening. "Yes?" she uttered softly, attempting to catch a glimpse of several people on her doorstep through the narrow opening.

"Ms. Miller?" I spoke.

A pause. "Who's asking?" came a cautious reply.

"Matt Duggan. I'm the private investigator assigned to locate Harold Mitchell, the missing scientist at Virolabs. I'm here with my assistant, Delia Perez, and a colleague of Harold's, Wayne Hutchinson. We would like to speak with you—if that's okay."

Making more of an effort to confirm the party of three through the narrow opening, she noticed Wayne Hutchinson standing behind Delia.

"It's me, Joan," he said as they made eye contact.

She removed the security chain from its slider. "Come in," she invited, opening the door.

I entered first. "Thank you, Ms. Miller. This is my assistant, Delia Perez. And I believe you and Mr. Hutchinson are already acquainted. We'll try to make this brief."

"And that's all it's going to be . . . BRIEF!" Hutchinson suddenly shouted. Stepping back several paces and holding an East German Makarov semi-auto pistol, he ordered Delia and me to lean forward against the living room wall. After taking possession of my revolver and cell phone, he instructed Miller to confiscate Delia's purse.

"Now what?" Miller asked, exchanging glances with Hutchinson.

"We're going to have to kill them, just like we did with Mitchell and those two fools of his," Hutchinson angrily replied, handing her my revolver. "They know all about your East German background, including your association with the research facility in Leipzig."

"What else do they know?"

"Whatever Mitchell told them before he had a chance to test his virus on these two. They knew where the vials were kept before we got there and moved them back to the lab. Just like that nosey neighbor we had to silence after she spotted us at Mitchell's home."

"Arrangements with our client will be much more difficult without test results," Miller insisted.

"I know that," Hutchinson snapped. "You can thank Mitchell for that blunder."

"Forget it," Miller said. "We'll deal with that later. First things first, starting with these two." Looking through Delia's purse, she retrieved her cell phone, removed the battery, then threw both on the floor. "Ahh, look what else Duggan's partner has in her purse—*handschellen*, as we call them in German." She handed the cuffs to Hutchinson. "I can handle Veronica Mars here. Place these bracelets on our clever detective so he doesn't give us any trouble."

"You'll never get away with it," I shouted, purposefully leaning as close to the wall as possible. I could feel the texture of the wallpaper through the palms of my hands.

"Shut up," Hutchinson snapped. He tucked his semi-auto pistol into his waistband. Miller simultaneously placed the barrel of the revolver against the back of Delia's head. "Try anything funny and your partner dies instantly. Understand?" he snarled.

"Whatever you say," I scoffed, turning my head and facing Delia, both of us making eye contact. She returned my wink.

Hutchinson opened the cuffs and grabbed my left wrist. In an instant Delia dropped to the floor, still facing the wall. She reached behind and grabbed Miller by both ankles and pulled. Miller fell, and the back of her head struck the tiled floor. Distracted by the commotion, Hutchinson dropped the cuffs and reached for the pistol in his waistband. I wheeled around and delivered a jaw-breaking punch to the side of Hutchinson's face. Both now lay unconscious, face up on the tile. Grabbing the guns and rolling both over, I cuffed Hutchinson's hands behind him. Delia bound Miller's wrists using a roll of masking tape found in a desk drawer.

"Should we contact Morelli?" Delia asked.

"Not before we search the house. It's obvious they were planning on delivering the virus to someone. I'd like to know who that *someone* is."

"You mean the so-called 'client' Miller was referring to?"

"Exactly."

"Hold on," Delia whispered after glancing out the front window. "A black and white just parked behind your car out front."

I glanced at Mitchell and Miller. "These two are out cold; they're not going anywhere. We can't ignore the two cops—let's go outside and see why they're here."

Walking out the front door and down the winding driveway, we approached the two policemen, now walking behind and around my vehicle.

"Can I help you, officers?"

"Is this your vehicle?" the officer standing behind my car asked.

"It is. Is there a problem?"

"We received a call about an unfamiliar vehicle in the neighborhood. Do you reside here?"

"No, we—"

BOOM. Delia, the two officers, and I ducked instinctively behind the police cruiser. The house we had just moments before exited was now totally engulfed in flames.

"What the hell?" the first officer yelled.

Drawing his service revolver, the second officer screamed, "On the ground, both of you—NOW!"

* * *

Morelli turned and walked away from the two dispatched officers and their supervisor. "I've explained the situation—as much as they need to know," he said. "At this time, we don't know who triggered the explosion, or why, but I'm willing to bet the bigger fish involved in all of this was not happy with Hutchinson . . . or Miller."

"And as far as Matt and I are concerned—intended targets as well, or just collateral damage?" Delia asked.

"That's a question we may never know the answer to," Morelli speculated.

"I still don't understand why Hutchinson hired a private investigative agency to track down a co-conspirator, a colleague of his he knew had stolen the virus and was preparing to test it on Delia and me."

"The trio may have calculated that your disappearance and death would provide not only the results they were looking for," Morelli suggested, "but would more deeply involve the FBI to the point it would result in a distraction, and thereby allow for an easier conclusion regarding their 'arrangements' with whatever hostile foreign party or criminal organization they were associated with. The good news is we've kept the virus out of the hands of some very bad people. It's back at Virolabs where it belongs. We don't know who all these bad actors are, and we'll continue our investigation, but we're confident that all the players at Virolabs they were in cahoots with have now been identified."

"But at a tremendously high price," Delia piped up. "Highly educated, talented scientists who took a wrong turn somewhere along the road."

"Better than millions of other innocent people—

wherever that deadly pathogen's final destination was intended," I declared.

Delia gazed wistfully at Morelli and me. "There's still an innocent party we're all forgetting."

"And who would that be?" Morelli asked, a curious look appearing.

"Susan Caine, the murdered widow who resided a few homes away from Mitchell."

Morelli nodded. "Yes, from the investigation conducted, it appears she was the innocent party in all of this."

"That's where we can still be of help," Delia suggested. "I'll conduct a search for any surviving family members. It's possible they may have a claim against the estate of the three deceased Virolab employees. She turned and looked at Matt. You onboard with this?"

"Absolutely, I am . . . not to mention any possible liability exposure for Virolabs."

Walking away from the crime scene and navigating the gauntlet of numerous firefighting and rescue vehicles, police cruisers, and FBI government cars, we stopped alongside my vehicle. I shook hands with my FBI friend. "Business aside, Frank, are you ready for another round of golf, or some fishing, perhaps?" I looked at Delia. "You're invited as well."

Morelli nodded. "Sure, Matt, anytime—just let me know. By the way, sorry I was so hard on you," he admitted, "but you can be a real pain in the ass sometimes."

"Oh, really?" I quipped sarcastically. "It wouldn't be because I'm contentious, ignore your suggestions, your orders, and do things my way, would it?"

Morelli smirked. "Smart ass—always a smart ass. Get ready to get your butt kicked on the golf course. Oh, and by the way, Columbo, forensics determined the caliber of weapon used in the execution of Mitchell and his thugs. It was a 9mm."

"Hutchinson's Makarov. What a surprise."

Delia walked between the two men. She latched on to my and Morelli's arms. "Do you two ever stop aggravating one another?" Exchanging glances with both of us, she asked, "Which of you handsome fellows will be taking me to dinner?"

Morelli and I looked at each other, then shrugged.

"Awesome," she said, beaming. "Both of you."

THE END

THE CASE OF THE CONNIVING GUN MOLL

EPISODE IV

PROLOGUE

After a string of serial bank robberies goes unsolved, Private Investigator Matt Duggan is retained by frustrated bank executives and regulators to help locate and identify the gang responsible. During the course of the investigation, his keen eye catches a tangible clue, which ultimately reveals the identity of the only female member of the gang: a mysterious, beautiful, and seductive woman whose charms ensnare Matt in a deadly trap. Tag along with the wise cracking, sharp-witted, tough private investigator and his devoted assistant Delia Perez as they follow a trail of greed, betrayal—and stone-cold murder.

.

PART I

Rushing through the bank's business door, a heavily armed gang of five dispersed in several directions throughout the medium-size branch.

"This is a robbery! Everyone on the floor . . . NOW! Stay QUIET! Don't touch any buttons or anything else. Don't play the hero or do anything stupid. Keep your mouths shut and remain face down. Close your eyes and turn your head away. Do as you're told and nobody will get hurt."

Clutching an assault rifle, the leader and his primary accomplice planted themselves in the middle of the bank's main lobby. They were dressed in jeans, long-sleeve shirts and gloves, their heads covered with a three-hole ski mask.

The leader began shouting out commands. "Number one," he barked, gesturing to one of his accomplices then pointing to the bank customers and the main entry door, the signal to guard the lobby, several lobby customers, and the door. "Number two," he yelled out, gestured to another accomplice, pointed to bank officers with customers in their lobby offices, then moved his arm and finger in the direction of the tellers, another command to herd bank officer employees and their office customers behind the counter. "Number three," he shouted, and pointed another accomplice toward the location of the bank vault directly over and behind the center teller. Number three, the smallest member of the robbery team, sprinted quietly toward and hopped over a section of the counter, moving into a back room and toward the vault. The third accomplice reappeared seconds later, rendering a thumbs-up, confirming the vault was open and loaded with cash.

The leader placed a hand on the shoulder of his colleague standing next to him. "Go," he ordered.

Number four darted toward the counter, carrying five folded seabags under one arm, a semi-auto pistol in the other hand. Hopping effortlessly onto and over the counter, the perp scampered toward perp number three.

During the next several minutes, bandits three and four entered and exited the vault five times, each time carrying a stuffed seabag and tossing it over the counter and onto the floor of the lobby.

"Listen up," the leader shouted. "All those on the floor . . . on your feet . . . NOW!"

As the customers and employees were herded around the counter in the direction of the vault, the bank's main entry door suddenly opened, and a young adult woman entered. Dressed in a tank top, shorts, sandals, and wearing a pair of dark sunglasses, she waddled inside, focused and fidgeting with her cell phone. Before she realized what was happening, perp number one grabbed her by the arm and roughly shoved her toward the center of the lobby.

"Hey, what the—"

"Keep your mouth shut and don't turn around," the gunman threatened, pressing the business end of a short-barreled shotgun against the back of her head. Caught completely off guard, she nodded in terror.

"Okay, customers and employees . . . inside the vault!" the leader hollered. Herding the employees and customers into the industrial-size safe, the masked kingpin wheeled the heavy vault door around on its hinges, the door closing with a loud thud. He turned toward his gang. "Let's GO!"

Scrambling out of the vault area and around the counter, each member of the robbery crew grabbed a seabag, then darted out the front door. A dark-colored van with tinted windows screeched around the corner, coming to an abrupt stop in front of the bank. The gang's leader yanked open the rear door of the van and each perp threw their seabag inside before jumping into the cargo area and pulling the door shut. The van driver sped away, making pre-arranged left and right turns for several blocks before turning into an abandoned alleyway where a large moving truck was parked and waiting, its rear door open and loading ramps extended. The van driver slowed just enough to safely roll the vehicle up and into the back of the waiting truck. After shoving the ramps back into the undercarriage, the truck driver and his accomplice closed and latched both doors before running back to the cab. Both truck and van escaped into the bustling city.

Cutting the engine and turning on the inside lights, the bank bandits sat on the floor of the van around the stuffed seabags. The desperados removed their masks, revealing thug number three to be the only female member of the gang. She shook her disheveled blonde hair, allowing it to fall to her shoulders before exchanging glances with the leader. Both gave huge smiles.

"We pulled it off again, baby," he told her. "You did great . . . I'm proud of you."

The diminutive perp leaped into his arms, hugging him. They exchanged a quick kiss before he said, "How does a trip to Hawaii sound?"

* * *

Delia opened my office door just enough to poke her head inside, then quickly pulled back. "Sorry," she whispered, "I didn't know you were on the phone."

I smiled and gazed up at my assistant, then raised my hand, repeatedly pulling my fingers toward me. Delia tiptoed inside, pulling the door shut and quietly moving a chair away from the front of my desk before sitting.

"I appreciate the call, Jim," I went on, "but I wouldn't worry about it. On the other hand, if you continue to see the same vehicle, then call me back, and we'll go from there." A pause. "Thanks. I'm fortunate to have such an alert neighbor." Another pause. "Okay, I'll do that. And thanks again." I pulled the phone away from my ear, returning it gently to its cradle.

"What was that all about?" Delia asked, a curious expression appearing.

I snorted. "That was the neighborhood watch commando," I said. "He wanted to let me know about an unfamiliar vehicle that's made repeated forays into the neighborhood over the last hour. I told him to call back if it continues."

"The neighborhood watch commando?"

I pressed my lips together and nodded.

Delia furrowed her eyebrows. "Oh, yes," she finally recalled. "I remember you mentioning him some time ago. Isn't that Mr. . . . ?"

"That's him," I cut in before leaning forward. "What was it you were so eager to tell me earlier . . . before you caught me on the phone with the neighborhood watchdog?" I asked, changing the subject.

"Three people walked in just before I interrupted you,"

she answered. "They're waiting in the lobby."

"Who are they?" I asked, looking up at my assistant.

"A John Richardson with the American Bankers Association, Bernard Metzler with the Western Branch of the Federal Reserve, and Paul Morgan, Regional Vice President of New Corporate Bank."

I cocked my head to the side, resting my chin between my thumb and forefinger. "Did I hear you say New Corporate Bank?"

"You did. A third branch was robbed two days ago. All three robberies appear to be by the same gang."

"Yep, I saw it on the news. Figured the feds were already on it. It's been a federal crime to rob any national bank or state member bank of the Federal Reserve since 1934." I turned my head to the side again, meditating before returning a puzzled look. "I wonder what they want with me?" I coyly asked, giving a shrug and a wry smile.

Delia responded with her trademark beautiful smile. "What does anyone *ever* want with you?" she knowingly emphasized.

I snorted a confirming chuckle. "All right, let's go talk with those people."

PART II

"Police and the FBI have linked several recent bank robberies matching this gang's MO," the representative from the Federal Reserve began. "Speaking on behalf of my colleagues, we believe they're one and the same. This is our conclusion based on witness descriptions, the police and FBI investigation, along with corroborating surveillance video."

Morgan and Richardson bobbed their heads in agreement.

Sitting on the front corner of Delia's desk, my arms folded, I quietly listened, acknowledging with the occasional nod as each bank officer took turns adding additional details about the hold-ups. Ten minutes and several rounds later, the banking officials grew quiet.

I stood and took in a deep breath. "You've all been very thorough. So, my question to the three of you is: What is it you want from me?"

Exchanging glances with each other, the bank officers shuffled anxiously in their seats before casting their attention in my direction. "Very simple," the New Corporate Bank vice president answered, speaking for his two colleagues. "We would like to add your expertise to that of the FBI and local authorities and put an end to these serial robberies before a customer or employee is hurt . . . or worse, killed."

"So far, we've been very fortunate," Richardson chimed in.

I stood and paced the agency lobby in pensive thought, then stopped. "Considering I have a working relationship with the FBI and MPD," I began, "I'd say we're off to a good start." I wheeled in the direction of the seated bank executives. "Next would be a viewing of the surveillance video captured from every branch during a robbery in progress by this purported gang of five."

Metzler stood. "We're a step ahead of you, Mr. Duggan. Our IT people have compiled a combined surveillance video of three branches robbed within the last sixty days by what we believe is the same gang." Looking around, he asked, "Is there somewhere we can review this?"

I nodded. "My office."

* * *

"I'd like to propose a toast . . . to you . . . and to us," the attractive man in a tuxedo quietly announced. Standing, he lifted his champagne glass toward the elegantly dressed woman sitting across from him at the dining table. "Here's to living fast, loving hard . . . and never dying young. To absent friends, and to ourselves, as no one is likely to concern themselves with our welfare . . . now or ever."

A combined smile and flush suffused her cheeks, a response to the flattering proposal she just received. She stood, responding to his toast by extending her bubbling glass in his direction. She clinked her flute with his, then raised the sparkling bubbly to her lips, draining it with a noticeable swanky laugh. He paused, taking note of her chuckle, unable to determine if it was a happy acknowledgment—or a cynical mock.

"Enjoying the evening?" he asked dubiously.

With her eyes focused on his, she replied, "You know how to make a woman happy . . . does that answer your question?"

"This is the finest French restaurant in the city," he bragged. "I made sure of it before I called for reservations. Nothing's too good for the woman I love."

Beaming, she walked around the table, meeting her boyfriend where he stood. She deftly removed the champagne flute out of his hand and set both on the rosette tablecloth-covered dining room table. She put her arms around him, and into his ear she quietly whispered, "When are we leaving for Hawaii?"

* * *

"You're right, Mr. Metzler, it's the same gang . . . same MO . . . all three robberies," I opined after reviewing the video. "They exhibit a distinct pattern of operation and behavior. I agree they're the same party committing these robberies. I'm confident the FBI and MPD would also agree."

"And why is *my* bank the number-one branch in the crosshairs of these thugs?" Morgan ruefully joined in. "They've hit us three times now. Only one other bank has fallen victim to this gang of five, that I'm aware of."

I turned and gazed at my assistant. "You want to respond to that?"

Displaying her usual sunny smile, Delia stood and flipped the light on. "Be happy to," she said, walking to the office window and opening the mini blinds.

"Before Delia begins . . . who wants coffee?"

All three visitors nodded, simultaneously mumbling in the affirmative.

Returning from the kitchen with coffee mugs in hand, Delia began, "Barring the fact that these thugs have engaged in willful criminal behavior, it's also an unfortunate fact that New Corporate Bank meets most of the criteria for why some banks are robbed more than others: an increased number of branches in urban areas, more bank outlets and extended hours, more mini-branches—such as those found in grocery stores and big box retailers—and more sprouting up in commercial districts along major transportation corridors, and so on."

The three banking officials exchanged glances. "We don't disagree, Ms. Perez," Metzler replied, speaking on behalf of his colleagues. "It's an accurate reminder of what we already know. I believe Mr. Morgan was simply voicing the same frustration we all feel."

"Understood," I jumped in, standing next to Delia. I glanced over the three bank officials. "Any questions?"

After a moment of hesitation, Richardson stood and stared at the pensive investigator. "What do you propose?"

"I can tell you this. There's one thing you can usually count on: Bank robbers are predictable; they normally employ the same MO in successive robberies. It's often this repetition—the same number of people, the use of particular robbery methods, or the same disguise—that leads to their apprehension. The ID or arrest of a single member can lead to the apprehension of the entire gang—any physical evidence they leave behind, names mentioned during the robbery, a description of the getaway vehicle, and so on."

The banking officials nodded in quiet acknowledgement.

"Based on what we currently know, the wheels are turning regarding an investigative protocol," I continued. "First thing I'd like to do is talk with the employees who were on duty the day of those robberies."

"We'll make the arrangements," Metzler affirmed.

"Good. Also, I'd like to hold on to the copy of the surveillance video we just viewed."

Metzler nodded. "As long as you need it."

"What about the FBI and local police involvement?" Morgan asked.

"I'll take care of that. Any more questions?"

Exchanging glances, the three banking officials stood. Each sporting a grin, they shook hands and quietly thanked Delia and me before walking single file out of the agency.

Delia's radiant smile returned. "So, tell me about the 'wheels are turning' metaphor you were referring to?" she asked, curious.

I sipped some coffee, then paused. "Let's play the video again . . . this time on your laptop."

"Why on my laptop?"

"Because your computer was upgraded with the advanced enhance and zoom AI software," I reminded her. "It can pan, enhance, and sharpen individual frames. Let's view the video again."

Delia smiled. "You're right, I completely forgot," she confessed, another moment of total recall occurring. "A Geek Squad guy dropped by and loaded the software. He then showed me how to use it." She exited my office and walked back to her desk. Inserting the disc into her laptop's DVD drive, she selected the pan and zoom effect feature. "It's ready."

"Forward the video until you get to the most recent robbery," I said, walking toward Delia's desk.

She pressed the fast forward button on the remote. At the last robbery on the disc, she pressed the stop button. "Okay, we're there."

"Hit the play button."

We both stood, reviewing the video again as the hold-up played out inside the New Corporate branch.

"Pause the video."

Delia turned and stared at me. "Okay, it's paused . . . now what?"

"We're on the right frame. That masked gang member's left arm is extended. Do you notice anything?"

Focusing on the image, Delia muttered, "Yeah, now that you mention it, I do see what appears to . . . Could it be a bracelet of some kind? I didn't notice it previously."

"Could be. I thought I caught a vague glimpse of something around that perp's wrist."

"And you did that without your PI magnifying glass," Delia kidded, adding, "you've got a pretty sharp eye, Mr. Private Eye."

I chuckled. "Continue what you're doing. Let's see if there's anything unusual . . . anything that stands out."

Panning and enhancing the image of the gang member's wrist to its highest setting and resolution, Delia stopped, moving closer to the monitor. "Ay, caramba!" she shouted, stepping back. "I was right. It's a bracelet . . . it's a damn bracelet." Incredulous, she turned and locked eyes with me.

"Okay, it's a bracelet. What's all the excitement?"

Delia snickered. "That perp's a female."

PART III

"We have one more job to do, baby, then we'll go . . . I promise," he whispered.

She broke away from his embrace, her face twisted with frustration. "You promised a vacation . . . that we'd go to Hawaii, and you're backing out . . . again."

"I'm not backing out of anything."

With an angry stare, she snarled, "What's to say you won't come out with that same song and dance after the next job?"

"Pipe down," the gang leader pleaded, pulling an embarrassed face. He cut a glance at the occupied tables around him, concerned her anger might escalate into a dangerous rant about the robberies. Clamping a hand on his girlfriend's shoulder, the criminal mastermind forcefully guided her in the direction of the restaurant's elegant lobby and revolving front door.

"Monsieur, mademoiselle," their tuxedo-clad waiter called out, running after the couple as they made their way toward the dining room entry and adjacent lobby. "Do you not wish to order dessert?" he asked in a pleading tone, his English carrying a noticeable French accent.

Stopping, the gang's leader stuck his hand in his jacket pocket, removing a roll of washed one-hundred-dollar bills. Peeling three off the top, he handed the waiter the money. "Not tonight, thank you . . . perhaps next time," he muttered, his voice laden with irritation.

"Oui, monsieur," the waiter replied resignedly. Pivoting in the girlfriend's direction, the waiter clicked his heels lightly and rendered a slight bow before uttering, "Mademoiselle" in a polite show of courtesy before turning around and walking back toward the maître d'.

Her reactive half-smile rapidly evaporated with an abrupt about-face. "Why don't you—"

"Why don't you zip it," he fired back, cutting her off. Returning his hand to her shoulder, he again directed her toward the entrance and the restaurant's valet service.

Breaking free of his grip, she stopped and turned around. "I'm really pissed at you," she shouted.

"We can talk about it later," he growled. "In the meantime, shut your trap before you say something we'll both regret."

Settling down, they waited uneasily for the valet service to return with their vehicle.

He's lied to me for the last time.

* * *

"Female? How do you know?" I asked, curious.

"It's a Pandora bracelet . . . and it's loaded with charms," Delia noted. "I have two of those bracelets."

"Really? Have I ever seen you wear them?"

"Oh, puh-leeze," Delia scoffed. "You may have graduated top of your class as a private investigator, but at feminine elegance school, you were obviously dead last." A pause. "*Yes*, I've worn them here," she politely sneered. "The Pandora brand encompasses a variety of bracelets that you pair with your favorite charms."

I chuckled. "Well, now you know another reason why I'm single."

Delia shook her head and smirked. "We'll skip that topic. In the meantime, I will again demonstrate my value as your assistant."

Rendering a wry smile, I folded my arms and nodded. "You have my undivided attention."

"Take a close look at the enhanced frame," Delia pointed out, sitting at her desk. "Notice the charms attached to the bracelet?"

"Yeah, I see them," I said, moving closer to the computer screen and squinting. I moved away from the monitor and gazed at my assistant. "So, talk to me . . . what is it?"

Delia opened her desk and removed a knife letter opener. Using it as pointer, she touched the screen, resting the knife end over one particular charm. "This is one of Pandora's newest charms for the current year . . . it's called the entwined hearts double dangle charm."

I nodded. "All right, I'm with you . . . continue," I said, moving toward the monitor for another look.

"There's only one retailer locally that carries that new charm, and it's in the Belford Mall. A friend of mine works there. I happened to be at the mall a few days ago to drop off a bracelet with a broken clasp, and to say hello. While I was there, she showed me their newest collection. And that charm was one of several she laid out on the glass counter."

Moving away from the monitor, I turned and faced my assistant. "Hmm," I murmured, pensive. "Do you think you can talk your friend into—"

Delia quickly placed her open hand in front of my face. "We go back a long way, Matt. And trust me . . . she owes me one."

I chucked. "So you're telling me it's time to collect on whatever mess you helped her out of?"

"Something like that," Delia said. "Remind me to fill you in . . . later." Glancing at the keyboard, she tapped in the command to shut down her computer, then opened a desk drawer and grabbed her purse and keys. Standing, she pivoted in my direction.

"Going somewhere?"

Delia smiled. "There's another charm out there . . . with my name on it."

PART IV

"She shops here frequently," the sales associate divulged in response to Delia's questions. Perusing a file of purchase orders, the associate stopped and removed the only two contracts for recent purchase of the entwined hearts double dangle charm, placing the paperwork on the freshly wiped glass counter.

After completing a visual sweep of the store's interior, Delia pointed out several security cameras throughout the small jewelry shop. "Do you happen to have video of these two people?"

"Our cameras are on a twenty-four-hour loop," the store employee answered. Tapping the paperwork on the counter, she added, "and since the purchases were made several days ago, there wouldn't be any video of those two customers."

"Twenty-four-hour loop?" Delia exclaimed. "Are you serious?"

Delia's friend sighed. "Yeah, I know," she glumly admitted. "I've talked to the owner several times about it, but this is a mom and pop operation, and they just don't want to spend the money."

Shrugging, Delia quickly entered the name, address, and phone number of the two customers into her iPhone.

"Do you remember enough about them that you can provide a physical description?" she asked.

"Damn, girl," the sales associate said, "I could get fired for giving you the information I've already provided, not to mention civil liability the store owners could encounter. I owed you one, Del, but as far as I'm concerned, this makes us even."

Delia responded with a sheepish half-smile, then changed the subject. "Well, it's time for this girl to add another charm to her collection. Show me your newest inventory," she requested, gazing at the displays underneath the glass counter.

Relieved the questioning was over, the store associate removed several trays from underneath the thick glass display, placing each one on the counter. With her eyes still on the trays, she murmured, "One is an older lady . . . the other a younger female, thirty-something, shoulder-length blonde hair, about five feet, four inches, 110 pounds . . . pretty."

Smiling, Delia pointed to a particular charm. "Let me take a look at that one."

* * *

Throwing a suitcase onto the bed they shared, she quickly packed several dresser drawers of clothing. *He won't be away very long,* she thought, nervously glancing at her watch. She grabbed a pink duffel bag out of the closet, filling it with toiletries, makeup, perfumes, and other personal items. Pushing a nightstand away from the king-size bed, she kneeled on the floor and removed a wood panel, revealing a crawl space underneath the raised wood subfloor. Reaching down, she removed one of several seabags resting on a large tarp spread out on the ground underneath the bedroom. *My share of the loot*, she thought, returning the floor panel and sliding the nightstand back over it.

She wheeled around at the sound of a knock on the front door, then reached inside the duffel bag, removing a semi-auto 9mm Glock. Walking cautiously into the living room, her Glock at the ready, she yelled out, "Who is it?"

"It's Quick Cab Taxi. I'm here for a nine thirty pick-up," a male voice hollered through the door.

She breathed a sigh of relief. She had forgotten about her earlier call to the taxi company to send a cab. The knock on the door had caught her momentarily off guard. Peering through closed vertical blinds in the living room, she noticed a silver Toyota Avensis parked directly in front of the house next to the curb, the words *Quick Cab Taxi* etched on the side of the vehicle. The driver was a young male, approximately six feet tall, in his mid-twenties she guessed, standing in front of the door wearing a shirt with the taxi company logo and his name embroidered over the shirt pocket. He was checking his cell phone.

"Be right there," she yelled again, lowering the pistol and returning to the bedroom. She stuffed the Glock back into the duffel bag, then zipped both the bag and suitcase.

Returning to the living room carrying the suitcase and duffel bag, she set both on the floor, then opened the door. Wearing a light green bodycon dress with plunging neckline, she smiled seductively, her lips lusciously painted.

"Good morning, ma'am," the driver pleasantly greeted, returning his cell phone to his right front shirt pocket. "You called for a cab . . . nine thirty a.m.?" He grimaced at the rhetorical question.

A pause. "Wow, you're cute," she said flirtatiously, smiling and strolling over the young driver's face. "Would you be a darling and go into my bedroom and fetch that last bag on the floor?"

* * *

"Okay . . . what's her history?" I asked, driving toward the address provided by Delia's friend.

"Her name is Joan Russo," Delia began, reading from the state and FBI rap sheets printed before leaving the office. "She's thirty-four and has a lengthy criminal record. Born in this state. Petty theft, shoplifting, fraud, drug trafficking, assault . . . all the way to bank robbery. She's served time in the local jail, state pen, and federal big house. Doesn't say anything about gang affiliations. She's also known by her nickname Felony . . . and probably proud of it," she added.

"Not your usual churchgoing choir girl," I snorted.

"Her photo and physical description match what my friend at the jewelry store told me."

"I'll look at it when we arrive at the address."

"What are we going to do when we get there?" Delia asked. "We can't just go barging inside and arrest her for bank robbery. We don't even know who else might be there. The last thing we need is a Bonnie and Clyde shootout right in the middle of a residential neighborhood."

I craned my head toward Delia and grinned. "Observation and investigation . . . like good private investigators," I replied in a sardonic tone.

Delia chuckled. "I'm reminded of the term *keyhole investigators.*"

I laughed. "Oh, you mean court papers the old PI firms of Slip, Trip, and Skip served perps through the keyhole back in the day?"

"Yes, exactly," Delia howled.

Adjusting the volume on my cell phone, I followed the voice instructions provided by the GPS. "Our computer search before we left the office confirms it's a single-family home, owned jointly by Jeffrey and Gretchen Moore. We'll park slightly before the house and across the street. You remain in the car with your cell phone ready to shoot video. I'll walk to the front door and ring the bell; when someone answers, I'll present myself as a local real estate agent and morph right into my phony song and dance asking if they know of anyone who might be interested in listing their home for sale."

"And I'll take video of whoever answers the door?" Delia knowingly asked.

"That's a rhetorical . . . yes."

Twenty minutes later I turned onto the destination street. Slowing to idle speed, Delia and I began our search for the house. "There." She pointed. "It's going to be that one . . . two houses ahead and on the right."

"The white bungalow with green trim?"

"Correct." Delia leaned forward, cupping her brow and squinting. "I can see the house number on one of the front porch posts."

I gently braked, then parked my vehicle next to the curb. I looked at Delia. "Ready to do this? Let me take a quick look at her mugshot on the rap sheet," I grunted, my assistant handing me the arrest record.

"I'm ready," she said, putting her iPhone in video mode. "This spot is perfect. I can make it look like I'm checking or responding to text messages or emails like most people do when staring at their cell phone . . . in case the occupant or anyone else notices."

I smirked. "I'll keep whoever answers the door so busy with my real estate babble, the only thing they'll want to do is get rid of me."

"Sounds like a plan."

I stepped out of the car and walked around the front of the vehicle and onto the sidewalk, ambling down the pavement and toward the house. Delia checked her phone again. "Okay, we're good to go," she mumbled.

* * *

The cab driver came to a stop underneath the hotel's porte-cochere. Exiting the vehicle, he opened the rear door, helping his alluringly attractive passenger exit the back seat. He walked to the rear of the cab, unlocked the trunk, then removed the suitcase, duffel bag, and the noticeable olive-green seabag, setting each on the concrete curb in front of the hotel's main entrance. "Anything else I can do for you, ma'am?" the exuberant taxi driver asked.

Flashing a disarming smile, the voluptuous young woman placed her hand on the driver's arm. "Yes, there is one more thing you can do for me, handsome," she purred in a sultry tone. Removing three one-hundred-dollar bills out of her purse, she gently took hold of his hand and turned it upward, placing the bills into his palm before closing his fingers with a gentle squeeze. "You've never seen me . . . understood?"

He gawked at her like a deer in the headlights.

Standing on her tiptoes, she reached up, placing her hand behind his neck, pulling him toward her. She pecked a gentle kiss on his cheek. He could smell the fragrant perfume coming from her perfectly toned body. She stepped back. "Did you hear me? You've never seen me before," she repeated.

"Uh, yes . . . oh, yes ma'am," the young driver stuttered

as if coming out of a trance, his eyes glazed over.

She smiled in approval. "Good . . . now be a darling boy and run along."

Turning around, she noticed several porters talking near the hotel's main entrance.

"I need a bellhop."

PART V

The driver of the caviar-colored two-door Lexus turned the street corner, the luxury car slowly making its way toward the asphalt driveway in front of its intended dwelling. The operator noticed someone approaching the same home, on foot—the one he resided in.

Who the hell is that? He stopped parallel to the curb, unaware the visitor's vehicle was parked several houses in front of him.

* * *

Pushing the doorbell button, I could hear the muffled two-toned chime. After waiting the usual length of time, I pressed the button a second time, followed by a light knock on the door. After another minute, I leaned in with my face pressed against one of two decorative side door windows, both with venetian blinds and both partially closed. No lights were on, and there was no indication of activity.

Either no one's home, or they're not answering the door. Completing an about-face, I sauntered down the concrete steps and onto the walkway. Strolling back toward my vehicle, I opened the driver's-side door.

"No one's home," I grumbled, slipping behind the driver's seat.

"Or maybe someone didn't want to answer the door."

"My gumshoe instincts are telling me no one's there."

"So now what?" Delia asked.

"We contact the owners," I said, pulling away from the curb and onto the residential street. "The landlord might be helpful . . . if we couch our approach and questions carefully."

* * *

Waiting for the unknown visitors near the end of the street, the Lexus driver moved away from the curb, knowing the vehicle in front would have to stop at the T-junction ahead. Careful not to accelerate, he allowed his vehicle to slowly close the distance behind the unfamiliar car.

"Got it," he mumbled, memorizing the plate number.

Turning in the opposite direction, the luxury car driver removed his cell phone from its mounted holder. Calling a recent number, he said, "Hey, I need a favor . . . run this tag number and get back to me. Get it done today."

* * *

"Like I've already said, I really don't know that much about the tenants," the owner of the home told Delia over the phone. "My property manager handles all those details. So, what's this all about?"

"Well, my colleague and I were driving through the neighborhood today," she explained in a cheerful tone, "and your home really caught our attention. I had no idea it was being rented until you mentioned it."

"I leased it for the first time two weeks ago to these tenants via the property management company. Hmm . . . you said no one answered when you rang the doorbell?"

"Yes . . . uh, I mean no," Delia replied, correcting herself. "No one answered. My colleague and I figured you and your family were off to work, school, et cetera. We just wanted to introduce ourselves and—"

"Wait a minute," the owner abruptly interrupted. "A neighbor friend of mine called earlier and mentioned something about a Quick Cab Taxi parking in front of the home and helping a woman leave the house with several bags. He also said he saw a man standing on the front porch shortly afterward. Was that your colleague?"

Delia swiveled her chair around, glancing at me. I was leaning against the door frame of my office and listening to the conversation. She grinned, adding a thumbs-up gesture.

Pushing away from the door frame, I walked around the front of her desk. I was eager to hear the news.

"Uhm . . . uh, yes, Mr. Moore," she replied. "And that explains why no one answered the door. Well, thank you for the chat." She began speaking hurriedly. "You and your wife certainly own a lovely rental home. It was nice talking to you, but I've got to run . . . thanks again for your time."

"Hey, hold on a minute," the owner of the home pleaded. "You haven't mentioned your name or the name of your—"

Delia gently placed the receiver back in its cradle.

"Great job," I said, lightly clapping my hands. "I could see your smile and feel your charm right over the phone. Now you know why I wanted *you* to talk to the owner."

Delia chuckled. "It took longer to find his phone number than our conversation lasted," she said.

"So, what did Mr. Moore tell you that put such a revealing smile on that lovely face?"

"According to a neighbor that called, our suspect left in a Quick Cab Taxi about half an hour before we arrived."

That's interesting, I mused. "Sounds like something my neighbor would do."

"You mean Jim, your neighborhood watch commander?"

"I should introduce those two," I said sarcastically. I rubbed my chin, pensive as I walked aimlessly around the front of the office. "Quick Cab Taxi? Hmm, I'm somewhat familiar with the owner. She drove my former partner home from our favorite watering hole on a few occasions when he had one too many."

"Seth?"

"Yeah . . . Seth," I replied in a sullen tone.

Delia pursed her lips, aware the mention of my former partner brought to mind unpleasant memories regarding his murder. "You plan on paying a visit to the owner of the cab company?"

I nodded. "Time for yours truly to employ his subtle blend of wit and charm."

Delia rendered a sideways glance. "Wit and charm?"

My mouth twitched slightly, followed by a cheesy grin.

Delia raised an eyebrow. "Oh, I get it . . . So, what's her name?"

"Fonda Petting, a former dancer and burlesque club owner."

"Oh, puh-leeze," Delia snickered.

PART VI

"The car is registered to a Matt Duggan. I did a little more checking. Are you ready for this? He's a private eye," the caller reported.

The Lexus driver jerked his head. "Holy shit . . . hold on a sec," he responded, tossing his cell on the passenger seat before turning into a run-down strip mall. Parking his car in the shade of a large palm tree, he reached down and retrieved the phone. "Did I hear you say . . . Matt Duggan?"

"That's what I said . . . Why, do you know him?" the caller asked.

"Let's just say that in our line of work, word gets around regarding certain cops and private dicks. Unfortunately for him, that's going to be a problem."

"What do you mean?"

"It means I caught Duggan snooping around my home."

"You want me to take care of it?"

"No . . . I'll deal with him soon enough. He's likely done nosing around for the day . . . at least at the house. I'll swing back around after dark. Sit tight with your phone . . . I may need you later."

"Okay, boss."

Ending the call, the Lexus driver rubbed his forefinger

against his top lip, pondering the implications of Duggan's involvement in unison with his girlfriend suddenly MIA. *Hmm, super sleuth shows up at the door, but not the cops or the feds? That tells me the boys in blue and J. Edgar don't know much—if anything—and Duggan's just snooping. If Joan was there, she pretended not to be, until he left.*

Pausing, he took in a breath before slowly exhaling. *If not, where the hell is she . . . and why isn't she returning my calls?*

* * *

"Thank you," the sultry young blonde whispered to the bellhop. At her direction, he removed her suitcase and bags off the luggage cart, setting them on the floor in the center of the suite. Acknowledging a generous tip with an appreciative smile, the attendant exited the room, pulling the door shut.

Ten minutes later the phone rang. The digital display confirmed it was the lobby desk.

"Hello."

"Hello, Ms. Russo," the front desk clerk chirped. "We're extending a courtesy call to ask if your room and our service have been satisfactory."

"Yeah, everything's been peachy," she drawled.

"Wonderful," the caller replied. "If there's anything further we can do to make your stay more comfortable, please do not hesitate to—"

"Yes, as a matter of fact, there is," she broke in. "I was about to make dinner reservations for early this evening. You can do it for me. Which of your restaurants do you suggest?"

"Our resort offers several exquisite dining experiences, Ms. Russo," the caller continued in a cheerful tone. "I would personally recommend Season's 52, our fine dining restaurant located inside the main villa. Would you like for me to make the reservation?"

"Make it for seven," she said.

"Consider it done, Ms. Russo. Is there anything else I can help you with?"

"Thank you. I'll let you know," she replied, hanging up the phone. Walking around and admiring the lavishly decorated room, she placed the suitcase on top of the king-size bed, then threw the seabag onto a large luggage rack. She grabbed the pink duffel bag stuffed with her personal care products and set it on the decorative marble top next to the sink and vanity adjacent to the bathroom. Grabbing her purse, she began digging through it, removing one of several fake passports.

"Bingo," she shouted, a shifty smirk appearing.

* * *

"His name is Denny Lovato," the owner of the cab company divulged. "He's one of my part-time drivers . . . a really nice young man. I dispatched him to pick up that particular fare after she called for a cab. She didn't inform him of her destination until she was in the back seat."

"Where did he take her?"

"To the Ocean View Resort . . . our drivers are required to complete and submit a waybill at the end of their shift. You can talk to Denny if you like. He's in the back, behind the building. Oh, and by the way . . . you and I never had this conversation."

"Understood . . . and thanks. I owe you one."

"You don't owe me a thing," the voluptuous brunette replied. "I haven't forgotten the clientele you and your partner funneled in my direction when I left the burlesque business and opened up this hackney service." She looked at me with a gentle but sad expression on her face. "I was devastated when I heard about your partner. He was a good guy . . . I liked him."

I nodded, appreciative. "Thanks, Fonda. That means a lot."

Smiling, she placed her hand gently on my forearm. "My name is Julie," she whispered softly. "Let me know if there's anything else I can do."

* * *

Waiting until dark, the Lexus driver turned slowly onto the street where he resided. Parking next to the curb several houses away, the gang leader exited his vehicle and headed toward the leased home. *No lights on.*

Unlocking the front door, he walked cautiously inside. *Where's Joan? What the hell is going on?*

Even in the dark, nothing appeared out of the ordinary—nothing, that is, until he walked into the bedroom and opened their closet door. "Damn, her clothing is gone," he mumbled.

Stepping out of the closet, the kingpin checked their dresser, quickly confirming her side of the dresser drawers were empty. *Shit.*

Alarmed, the gang boss removed a small flashlight from the nightstand next to their king-size bed before moving it away from the adjacent wall. Kneeling, he removed a section of false flooring, revealing the same crawl space underneath the home where the stolen loot was hidden. Aiming the flashlight at the seabags, the gang's mastermind noticed one was missing. He took in a deep breath, then pressed his lips together before angrily muttering, "God dammit, I'll kill that bitch."

* * *

"Her name is Joan . . . uh, let me think . . . uhm, yeah . . . Joan Russo. That's the name I heard when she was on her cell phone while on the way to the Ocean View Resort. I guess it was in reference to reservations she made or was making to stay there," Denny Lovato surmised, standing next to his cab in the parking area just behind the cab company's call center.

"We appreciate your help," I said, patting the driver on the shoulder.

Sporting a smile and with a quick shake of his head, Denny confessed, "To be honest, I thought she was gorgeous . . . and I liked the way she talked to me." Exchanging his smile for a serious look, he asked, "Why? Is she in some kind of trouble?"

"That's what we're trying to find out," Delia said, "so it's really important our conversation remains confidential . . . until this is all sorted out."

He nodded. "Yeah, I get it."

"Is this her?" Delia asked, handing the cab driver the mugshot she printed from the police rap sheets.

Denny gazed at the photo. "Yeah, that's Joan," he sighed while nodding, "but the photo doesn't do her justice . . . if you get my meaning."

"I get it," Delia replied, flashing a smile.

"Are we done?" Denny asked, a somber note in his voice.

I pursed my lips and gave an appreciative half-smile. "Yeah, we're done . . . and thanks again."

Returning to my vehicle, Delia and I stopped, then faced each other.

"Ready to peep through some keyholes?" I asked, a mischievous grin appearing.

"Dirty old man . . . you would think of that," Delia teased.

"A metaphor for some old-fashioned surveillance," I explained. "Odds are our suspect is still there. We may catch her milling about. That's the beauty about resort hotels: There are restaurants, shops, conventions, parties . . . a whole host of activities that continue into the night. It's doubtful she'll hunker down in her room all evening. She'll want to check it out."

Delia revealed a coy smile. "Speaking of restaurants, it so happens a friend of mine told me about this really nice restaurant inside the—"

"Yeah, yeah, I know . . . dinner," I snickered.

PART VII

Decked out in a new summer floral dress, Joan Russo pulled the door of her hotel suite shut. She hooked the bright red DO NOT DISTURB sign over the room's lever door handle before strolling seductively down the hallway toward the elevator lobby. Glancing at herself in a full-length mirror on the wall opposite the elevator, she admired and smiled at her reflection. *Cute, very cute,* she thought, whirling around several times. The dress flaunted her shape, accentuated further with a pair of knee-length boots and a floppy sunhat. It was a boho-chic look designed to facilitate browsing around, window shopping, and later, dinner.

"Beautiful," she heard a voice utter in the background.

Joan turned to see a middle-aged male sauntering down the hallway and past the elevator lobby. Voicing his approval with a confirming grin, he had caught sight of the young woman checking herself in the mirror. Returning a smile, she walked into the voice-activated elevator. "Lobby," she uttered.

* * *

"Hello, Mr. Moore . . . this is Davin Ferrante. How are you this evening?" the unfamiliar caller politely asked.

"I'm sorry . . . Who is this?" Jeffrey Moore repeated.

Pulling the cell away from his ear, Ferrante quickly glanced at the screen. *Yeah, this is the correct phone number*, he thought. "Davin Ferrante," the caller said again. "My girlfriend and I are the new tenants in your home in Coyote Creek."

"Uhm . . . oh, yes . . . yes. Now I remember. Sorry about that. The property manager normally handles any issues or problems regarding the house. You'll need to give them a call and—"

"That's not why I'm calling," Ferrante abruptly cut in.

A pause. "Okay, if it's nothing involving the home, then what can I do for you?" Moore asked.

Placing his cell phone in speaker mode and setting it on the kitchen counter, Ferrante opened the refrigerator and reached for a beer. "I understand someone dropped by earlier today," he went on, "but no one was here. I mean we just moved in, and people we don't even know are already banging on the front door."

Moore sighed. "I understand your concern, and I'm terribly sorry. It was a couple of pesky real estate agents looking for a new listing. Coyote Creek is prime real estate . . . every brokerage in town would kill to list any house in that development."

"How do you know they were real estate agents?" Ferrante asked.

"Because they called me," Moore replied. "I was told no one answered the door, so they assumed the occupants had already left."

"Yeah, that's correct. The neighbor told me about it after I returned late this afternoon," he lied. "I could have saved you a call had we spoken to them."

"Oh, no problem. By the way, does your girlfriend

normally take a cab to work?" Moore asked, changing the subject.

Ferrante cocked his head. "What do you mean?"

"That same neighbor called earlier and told me a cab dropped by about half an hour prior to the arrival of the real estate agents. He said the driver helped a young blonde female load several bags into the vehicle before departing."

Ferrante choked back his anger, then faked a chuckle. "Oh, uh, yes, I completely forgot," he lied again. "My girl-friend had a flight to catch on behalf of the company she works for. Unfortunately, I had to leave earlier, and I was unable to take her to the airport, so she must have made those cab arrangements with . . . if I remember correctly, uhm . . . Pinpoint Cab Company."

"Hmm . . ." Moore mumbled. "I believe the neighbor said it was Quick Cab Taxi."

* * *

"Wow, this *is* beautiful," Delia gasped, checking out the polished resort as we strolled leisurely underneath the enclosed glass atrium. Offering nightly entertainment, on-site boutique shops, four restaurants, a cafe and several bars, the resort dazzled her.

Captivated by the interior landscaping, I couldn't help but feel drawn by its curb appeal. "I'd like to know who came up with the landscaping designs," I marveled, looking around.

"And this is just a small portion of Ocean View Resort," Delia remarked. "There's a sand beach area, waterfall, and—"

"And we have a suspect we're supposed to be looking for," I interrupted, turning and facing my assistant. "This is all very glamorous and appealing, but let's not forget why we're here."

Delia gave a resigned smile. "You're right . . . we're getting a little too caught up in the moment. We need to focus on spotting Russo." She turned in the direction of the main lobby. "Sure would make things easier if we could—"

"It would. Unfortunately, we can't," I interrupted again. "But there is something we *can* do."

"Okay," Delia whispered, returning a curious look. "And what would that be?"

I checked my watch. "It's almost dinner time. What's the name of that restaurant your friend recommended?"

Delia smiled. "Season's 52."

PART VIII

Parked in front of the call center, Davin Ferrante kept watch on the short alley flanking both sides of Quick Cab Taxi. Signs posted denoted the entrance and exit for the only two vehicles owned and operated by the small cab company.

Several minutes into cooling his heels, a taxi slowed and turned into the entrance alley.

"Good, he's back . . . he'll be outta there with a new fare in short order," Ferrante quietly grumbled. He knew the cab's return, for whatever reason, would be a quick pit stop. *Parked cabs generate zero revenue,* he mused.

Less than five minutes later, the same cab — or its twin — bolted out of the alley exit and onto the main thoroughfare.

The gang leader smiled. "Bingo."

* * *

Stepping behind Delia, the maître d' pulled a chair away from their assigned restaurant table, gently pushing it back as she prepared to take a seat. "Thank you," she acknowledged. I sat myself opposite my assistant.

"Beautiful restaurant," I commented, surveying the inside of the eloquent steakhouse. The environment was ambient, with a relaxed atmosphere, candlelit tables, and soft background music playing.

"Your server will be right with you. Enjoy your evening," the head waiter said cordially, offering a departing smile before completing an about-face and returning to the reservation podium.

"You're right. It *is* beautifully decorated," Delia said.

Arriving only moments after the departure of the maître d', our server appeared. Smiling, she stood next to the table holding a pair of à la carte menus in her arms. "Hi, I'm Natalie," she greeted, "and I'll be your server this evening." Handing the menus to Delia and me, she took a step back. "Would either of you care to order anything from the bar?"

"No, I don't think..." I began, but stopped mid-sentence. I caught a glimpse of someone out of the corner of my eye entering the restaurant, then turned and looked at Delia. Craning my head slightly and glancing up at the waitress, I politely asked, "Can you excuse us for a moment?"

The server pursed her lips and nodded. "Certainly," she said, turning and walking toward another occupied table.

"What is it?" Delia asked.

I maintained eye contact with her. "I think our suspect just walked inside," I murmured. "Without making it too obvious . . . tell me quietly what she's doing," I whispered, pointing with my gaze.

Shifting in her seat and peeking discreetly in the direction of the alleged culprit, Delia observed the woman speaking inaudibly with the maître d', her back facing our table. "She's at the podium, probably confirming a reservation or asking for a table."

"Okay, keep watching her," I whispered.

The young woman finally turned and walked away, strolling in the direction of the restaurant's bar and out of our line of sight.

"She walked into the bar area," Delia said. "Maybe she wants a drink before she's seated in the main dining area."

"You said she walked into the bar?"

Delia snorted a soft chuckle. "I'd probably do the same thing if I were in here solo," she answered.

I leaned back in my chair, pondering. "Hmm, it might just work," I mumbled, staring blankly in the direction of the podium.

Delia gave a curious look. "What might work? What are you talking about?"

"She has no clue we're surveilling her."

"Okay . . . and?"

"My use of flattering language," I said, grinning. "You know, the kind of talk certain men use to persuade a woman to do something."

Delia made a face. "You mean you're going to . . . hit on her?"

"Exactly."

* * *

After tailing the cab for several miles, Ferrante pressed the brake pedal in response to the driver slowing and turning into the parking lot of a popular sports bar. Following the operator into the parking area, he stopped behind the taxi, hurriedly exiting his vehicle and walking headlong toward the driver's side door.

Startled, the young cab driver looked up from the driver's seat, the door window rolled down. "Can I help you?"

Returning his surprised gaze with a blank expression, Ferrante snatched the door open. Bending down, he reached inside and yanked the driver out of the car.

"Hey man . . . what the hell?" Denny cried out.

"You listen to me . . . and you listen good," Ferrante growled, holding the taxi driver by the scruff of his shirt collar. "How many drivers have been on duty today?"

"Wha . . . what?" the confused cab driver replied. "I'm just here to pick up a fare. Did I do something . . . cut you off . . . not signal . . . what?"

Ferrante shoved the bewildered driver against the side of the vehicle. "I'm not going to ask you again." He pulled a semi-auto pistol out of his pocket and jammed it into Denny's temple.

"Uh . . . uh, only one," he stuttered, trembling with fear and confusion. "Wha . . . what's this all about?" Denny jabbered.

Hovering over the terrorized driver, the gang chieftain, snarled, "You were dispatched to a house early this morning and picked up a woman by the name of Joan Russo. Does that ring a bell?"

Denny nervously nodded.

"Where did you take her?"

Paralyzed with fear, Denny mumbled incoherently.

Pressing the gun barrel harder into his temple, Ferrante grew angrier. "Go on . . . tell me where you took her."

"Uh, to . . . uh, to the Ocean View Resort."

Ferrante leaned back, feeling as smug as a raffle winner. "Thanks," he said with a smirk before smashing his gun into the side of Denny's skull. After shoving the unconscious driver over to the passenger side, he stepped in behind the wheel and parked the cab within a darkened L-shaped corner. Moving the front seat back as far as it would go, the gang kingpin bound and gagged Denny, then pushed him face down on the floorboard. Returning to his

Lexus, he grabbed his cell phone lying in the center console, locating and pressing a contact number.

"Yeah boss," came the reply.

"Round up the boys, then drive to the Ocean View Resort. Give me a call when you arrive. We'll meet in the parking lot."

"What about Joan?"

Ferrante chuckled. "She's already there. We're gonna throw her a little surprise party."

* * *

I made my way to the bar area and immediately spotted the suspect seated on a high barstool. I watched as she ordered a cocktail. Lighting a cigarette, she swiveled her seat for a better view, waiting for the bartender to return with her drink. Her leather boots resting on the stool's base ring made her appear taller than she was. She reached for her small purse on the counter, a black leather Gucci mini bag complete with a monogram gold-toned double G on the flap. As she fumbled with the purse, it slid off her skirt, falling to the floor.

"You dropped this." I smiled, appearing out of nowhere. I handed the suspect's purse back to her.

"Thanks," she whispered, caught off guard by my sudden appearance.

"You're welcome. It's not often I have the pleasure of returning a beautiful woman's purse back to its rightful owner."

She chuckled at my reply. "Well, as the phrase goes, chivalry isn't dead . . . at least not totally."

I gave a slight bow. "I'll take that as a compliment."

She exhaled a thick cloud of smoke from her cigarette.

"It was intended as a compliment."

I glanced at the bar stool next to the suspect, then placed my hand on the chair's back rest. "Is this seat taken?"

Crossing her legs, she returned a coy smile, then swiveled her chair again in my direction. "It is now."

PART IX

"Nice . . . very nice," I noted, walking slowly around the hotel room, my wandering eyes probing Russo's elaborately decorated suite. I watched as she placed her Gucci purse on the mirrored dresser table in front of the king-size bed. Out of the corner of my eye I caught a quick glimpse of an olive-green seabag atop a suitcase rack, the same type of seabag I remembered seeing when I viewed the security footage provided by New Corporate Bank.

"Does the room meet your approval, Mr. Duggan?" she asked, noticing my eyes strolling over the suite.

"Makes my room look like a run-down boarding house by comparison," I mumbled. "Oh, and please . . . call me Matt."

"Okay . . . Matt." She smiled flirtatiously. "So . . . where *is* your room?"

"Steerage . . . with the rest of the peasants," I replied with a cynical chuckle.

Joan turned and looked at me, a puzzled expression appearing, but exchanged it for a dodgy smile. "Oh, okay, I get it . . . haha . . . the *Titanic*. You're a funny guy. I like a man with a sense of humor."

I exhaled a breathy laugh. "Well, I—"

She cut me off. "Why don't you stop talking . . . and

help me with my necklace," she teased in a seductive way, fiddling with the clasp behind her neck. Turning again and facing the mirror, she could see my reflection as I approached her from behind.

Gently touching her shoulders, I slowly moved my hands inward until I reached the necklace, quickly unhooking the clasp while she parted her hair with her hands. "Here you are," I whispered, lowering each end of the necklace, a slender 24-karat gold chain supporting a pendant which until now had gone unnoticed. It was the Pandora entwined hearts double dangle charm Delia had previously pointed out that caught my attention. I glanced at her right wrist, where the Pandora bracelet lay, complete with approximately ten other charms.

"Beautiful necklace and pendant," I commented.

Joan spun around. "I love you unconditionally," she said.

Caught off guard, I chuckled. "Really? Well, this certainly takes 'love at first sight' to a new level."

Her face broke into a wide grin. "That's the engraving on the charm, silly," she explained, placing her arms around me.

"Well, if that's the case, I'd be interested in seeing what the other charms on your bracelet—"

"You're just too handsome to be doing all this talking," she whispered seductively, cutting me off again. Our eyes met. I wrapped my arms around her slender waist, pulling her close. Bending down, I pressed my lips against hers, feeling a jolt of passion, until she peeled away.

I was surprised. Was she playing hard to get . . . or regretting the invitation to her room?

"Maybe we should go back to the lounge," she suggested nervously.

I cocked my head to the side. "Well, uh . . . sure, if that's what you'd like to do. Is something wrong?"

She turned and walked quietly around the king-size bed.

"You have an entire bar here in your suite, courtesy of the resort," I pointed out, heading for the mini wet bar. Several small refrigerators were tucked neatly below the counter. I stooped down to check out the inventory, muffling a quick "I can make us a drink if you like."

"Uh, sure, okay," Joan mumbled. Quietly pulling open the nightstand drawer, she reached inside.

"Ah, yes . . . here we go," I said, locating several bottles of premium vodka, bourbon, rum, and tequila. Grasping several bottles by the neck, I stood, placing each on the countertop. "Okay . . . so far, so good," I muttered. "Hmm, let's see . . . a couple of glasses . . . some mixers . . . and a few ice cubes." Satisfied I had what I needed, I said, "Okay, Joan . . . what's your pleasure?"

"Step around the bar . . . and do it slowly," came the gruff reply.

My head whipped around, my eyes fixated on the gun. I paused, flashing a nervous grin. "Wow, talk about ending a date on a not-so-positive note . . . So, what's with the gun?"

She stepped away from the nightstand. "I was just about to ask you the same question. And keep your hands away from your jacket."

"What are you talking about?" I blurted.

"I'm talking about the gun you're wearing. I felt it when you kissed me. All you male jerks think I'm the proverbial dumb blonde," she ranted. Her tone growing more menacing, she walked closer. "I know all about guns . . . and that wasn't your hand or your wallet brushing against my boob."

A cynical smile played around the corners of my mouth. "What can I say? Trust is in short supply these days. Everyone I know is packing."

"The only suits I know who are packing heat are the cops," Russo hotly replied. "Open your jacket opposite the side of the gun and remove your wallet. Do it now . . . and do it slow."

Complying with her order, I grabbed the front of my jacket containing my wallet and moved it out and away from my torso. Using my other hand, I slowly reached inside.

"Toss it on the bed. Do the exact same thing with the gun . . . throw it on the bed as well . . . then step away," she demanded.

Clutching the Glock and moving cautiously toward the king-size bed, Russo covered my gun with a pillow, then reached for the wallet with her free hand. Flipping it open, she stole a quick glance at the private investigator's license that appeared. Tossing the wallet back on the bed, she looked up at me.

"Does this mean our date is over?" I asked in a cynical tone.

"Shut up," Joan barked. "Cop, detective, private dick . . . you're all cut from the same cloth. You better start talking, mister, or you're a dead man walking. No one plays me for a fool."

* * *

Ferrante and his three thugs stopped at the resort's main entry. Surprised at the enormity of its size from the interior, they continued to gaze in astonishment at the gargantuan vacation and convention center.

"All right, so now what?" one of his goons asked,

unsure of how they would go about locating their accomplice and partner in crime.

"So now we find Joan," Ferrante sneered.

"How?" another perp asked. "This place is enormous."

"Joan loves swanky places like this. Knowing her as I do, she's checked in as a guest . . . and has a suite. Look." He nodded in the direction of the main lobby counter. "There's minimal traffic at all the check-in booths. You three keep those people busy. Since I'm the only one wearing a coat and tie, I'll slip behind the counter and find out what room she's been assigned to." He gave his associates a stern look. "Get moving."

"Okay boss," voiced a single reply, his criminal colleagues making their way toward the employee-staffed booths.

Ferrante proceeded toward the end of the lengthy counter; lifting the counter flap, he made his way back toward the office located behind the check-in booths. Stealthily opening the office door, he walked inside, pressing the lock button on the door handle before releasing it. A lone, middle-aged male employee sat at a desk in the center of the room, his face glued to a desktop computer screen.

"Can I help you?" the hotel employee asked, startled at the sound of the door slamming shut.

Ferrante displayed a cynical smile. "As a matter of fact, I believe you can," he announced, making his way toward the seated employee.

The resort hotel employee made an anxious face. "Are you new here? I don't believe I've seen you before."

"Well, uh, I suppose you could say I'm new . . . but only for a few minutes. The good news is there's just one easy thing I need for you to do."

The employee's face twisted in puzzlement. "Beg your

pardon . . . what's that?"

Reaching the desk, Ferrante removed his holstered Beretta. "I need the suite number of a guest. Her name is Joan Russo. And I know you can find it on that computer you had your face buried in just a few moments ago."

The employee swallowed hard. "The . . . the . . . that information is confidential," he stammered, his eyes locked onto the gang leader's pistol. "I'll be fired if I—"

Ferrante reached over and slugged the employee in the face with the barrel of the gun. "Correction—you'll be *dead*, and then you won't have to worry about being fired. Now give me the room number before someone knocks on the door."

Stunned by the blow, the terrified employee fumbled with the keyboard.

"You better cough up that room number in a hurry, mister, before you make this gun I'm holding really angry."

Panic-stricken, the hotel employee finally located the room number. "It's s-s-suite number 1116," he sputtered.

Ferrante pinched his lips together in a crooked half-smile. "Thanks," he said in a smug tone before walking behind the employee and bringing the full weight of the Beretta on the back of his head.

The gang leader bound and gagged the unconscious man before stuffing him inside an office supply closet and removing what appeared to be a master key card clipped to his belt. He noticed a box of magic markers on a shelf. *Just what I need*, he thought, using one to write the words DO NOT DISTURB on a sheet of printer paper. Exiting the office, he attached the taped note to the front of the door just as another employee prepared to walk inside.

"Oh, excuse me," she said, almost bumping into him. "I need to see Mr. Murray. I just finished locating the figures he wanted and—"

"I'm sorry," Ferrante replied in an apologetic tone. "Mr. Murray told me to leave this note on the front door. He's busy . . . unexpected conference call with corporate. As a matter of fact," he said, "the boss man just told me to take a hike. Looks like he'll be tied up for a while."

She tossed the folder of papers onto an adjacent credenza. "Well, here's the figures he asked for," she grumbled, "whenever he's ready for them." She looked around in frustration, her gaze finally returning full circle to the face of the strikingly handsome, but unfamiliar man she just encountered. "Are you new here?" she asked. "I don't believe I've seen you before. You're not wearing a name tag."

"Uh, yeah, I'm new . . . just started today. HR is taking care of my name tag," he lied.

Exchanging her previous look of annoyance with a now interested smile, she introduced herself. "I'm Katie . . . with the auditing department," she announced, extending her hand.

"And I'm busy," Ferrante barked, ignoring the employee's friendly gesture. Walking back in the direction of the counter flap, he stopped and pointed at the office door. "Oh, and a word to the wise . . . don't go in there."

Startled by the rudeness of this new employee, Katie lurched forward. "I have no intention of—"

"Who's that?" a colleague of Katie's interrupted. Both gawked at Ferrante as he walked quickly in the opposite direction.

"I don't know," she answered with an exasperated sigh. "He said he's new, but one thing I *can* tell you . . . he's a first-class jerk. I'd sure like to know how he charmed his way past Stone-Cold Medusa."

Katie's coworker laughed. "You mean the HR recruiting

manager? The one with the Shirley Temple pin curls that look like snakes?"

"He must have steamrolled right over her with a fake charm or bullshit dozer," Katie said.

"Hmm . . . too bad." Her coworker chuckled. "He sure is good looking, I'll give him that; but as my manizer sister is so fond of saying: He may be nice to look at . . . but handsome is as handsome does."

PART X

Delia glanced at her watch. *He walked out of the bar with that woman more than fifteen minutes ago,* she thought. *If this wasn't official business, I'd be pissed.* She let out a worried sigh. *I'd better go look around.*

Noticing Delia was now solo, the waitress returned, an awkward silence hanging over the table. "Uh, excuse me, ma'am, will your gentleman friend be returning? Can I get you anything?"

Pressing her lips together, Delia tapped her fingers thoughtfully on the table. She pushed her chair back and stood. "Uhm, no, but thank you anyway," she said nonchalantly, a smile now replacing her worried thoughts. "Oh, and here's a little something for your time," she offered, stuffing a twenty-dollar bill into the server's hand.

"But . . . you didn't order anything," the young woman quietly fussed, looking down at the folded bill.

Delia gave a slight smile. "You took good care of this table," she replied, turning and walking briskly toward the restaurant's egress.

Strolling past the pub, she caught sight of someone behind the bar waving a hand. "Excuse me, ma'am," a voice shouted out. "Can you hold up a minute? I have something for you."

Hesitating, Delia waited for the bartender to walk out from around the bar. Handing her a book of matches, he explained, "I was told to give this to you when you left the restaurant."

"You were told to give this to me?" she repeated. "By whom?" she asked, staring at the matchbook.

The bartender grinned. "By that gentleman you were sitting with earlier. He sure makes his way around . . . uh, no offense, ma'am. He's a good tipper . . . gave me an extra sawbuck for the matches. Easiest twenty I ever made." He chuckled. He began to head back to the bar before stopping abruptly and turning around. "Oh, and have a nice evening, ma'am," he added, turning again and walking back inside the bar.

Delia continued her puzzled stare at the matchbook, emblazoned with the image of the Seasons 52 Restaurant on the front and back cover. *I can't believe these are still being made,* she thought, remembering a time in the past when restaurant matchbooks were an advertising ploy and a tool for a post-meal cigarette. *Matt knows I don't smoke . . . or collect matchbooks. What was he thinking when . . .*

"Oh my God, wait a minute," she mumbled out loud. Opening the cover, she peeled it back and away from the matchsticks. Delia shook her head and smiled. Printed on the inside of the back cover was *Room 1116.*

* * *

"Let's go." Ferrante gestured to his minions, ordering them to cease their activity with the front desk clerks and come to him.

"You know where she is, boss?" the top henchman asked.

"Eleventh floor . . . suite 1116. I have a master key. She

may or may not be there."

"What's the plan?"

"Stay here and keep an eye on that door," he said, pointing toward the office door with the note attached. "If anyone enters or exits that room, grab your cell and call me." Ferrante craned his head in the direction of the two other perps. "You two start walking around. If you see Joan, don't let her out of your sight . . . and call my cell. Either way, I'll be back with the money."

"Okay, boss."

Ferrante strolled toward the closest elevator and walked inside, pushed the button for the eleventh floor, and waited for the doors to close before removing his holstered pistol. Pulling the slide back and chambering a round, the gang leader carefully returned the semi-automatic handgun back to its holster.

The elevator doors opened on the eleventh floor. He exited and followed the numbered rooms, finally stopping in front of Joan's suite. Grabbing his semi-auto pistol again, he slipped his other hand inside his outer jacket pocket and retrieved the master key, hearing the vague sound of conversation coming from inside. *Appears she has a visitor,* he brooded.

Passing the card key over the door reader, he heard a faint *click* before turning the handle, then slowly pushed the door open.

"I told you to shut up and sit down," he heard Joan yelling. The gang leader continued to make his way quietly through the foyer, both arms fully extended and clutching his pistol with both hands. Coming into view, he observed his girlfriend holding an unknown male at gunpoint. He was sitting in a chair.

* * *

"Put the gun down, Joan," Ferrante ordered, making himself visible as he exited the foyer and made his way into the suite's sitting area. He aimed the Beretta directly at his girlfriend. To me he said, "You . . . stay in your seat . . . do not move."

She whipped her head around. "Davin," she nervously cried out, a rueful grin appearing. "Oh my God, am I happy to see you."

"Yeah, I'll bet you are," he angrily replied. "I told you to put the gun down," Ferrante bellowed a second time. "I'm not going to tell you again."

"I think you should do what he says."

Joan returned a furious look at me. "Shut up . . . nobody asked you."

Ferrante cocked the gun.

"Okay . . . okay, Davin . . . whatever you say." Slowly stooping down, the gang leader's girlfriend gently placed her Glock on the carpeted floor.

"Now go sit on the bed." He motioned with his gun. Trudging in the direction of the Glock, he bent down and picked up the weapon, stuffing it into his waistband.

"Davin, I—"

"Who's your boyfriend?" he interrupted.

"Boyfriend? What are you talking about?" she asked in a disingenuous tone. "That's his ID wallet on top of the bed. He's a private investigator . . . or so the ID says."

Ferrante reached down and picked up the wallet, flipping it open. "Well, I'll be damned," he said, a maniacal grin making its way across his face. Shifting his gaze between me and the ID, he tossed the wallet back onto the bed. "It's the infamous Matt Duggan, Private Investigator in the flesh."

"So he's a private dick . . . what's the big deal? They're a dime a dozen," Joan said.

"The big deal is he's up here . . . in your room . . . with the money you stole," he barked, gazing at the seabag.

I uttered a sarcastic laugh. "That's a bit like the pot calling the kettle black, don't you think?"

Ferrante aimed his Beretta in my direction. "One more word out of you, and I'll decorate these walls with the insides of your head."

"What are we going to do?" Joan pleaded.

Ferrante gave a hollow laugh. "There is no more *we*, you dim-witted floozy. You ran off with the gang's money, checked into this ritzy hotel, then picked up Phillip Marlowe here like a dumb, cheap whore. He played you like a fiddle. He knows all about us, and the bank jobs. Do I have to spell it out for you? Are you that dense?"

"Davin, it's not what you think . . . believe me, I—"

"And if Duggan knows where *you* are . . . well, I'm not waiting around to find out." Ferrante hurried toward the suitcase rack and grabbed the seabag with his free hand. He turned and headed toward the foyer, dropping the bag on the floor.

"I'm going with you," Joan shouted, standing.

"You're not going anywhere," Ferrante fired back, wheeling around.

"Please, Davin, listen to me," she begged. "This is all a misunderstanding. I was going to call you . . . it's just that I—"

"Shut up," Ferrante shouted, gazing one last time at his elegantly dressed now ex-girlfriend. "You're just a glad rag doll, and a luxury I can no longer afford . . . or trust. Now turn around."

He's not leaving any witnesses, I thought. *If I can just . . .*

Joan let out a blood-curdling scream, distracting

Ferrante just long enough for me to launch myself off the bed and directly into the Brooklyn-born street thug and gang leader, knocking the Beretta out of his hand and underneath the bed. We both tumbled to the floor.

Russo scooped her purse off the dresser and ran for the door, grabbing the seabag full of cash on the way out. Reaching the floor lobby, she repeatedly pressed the down button on the control panel between the two elevators, one elevator opening after what seemed like an eternity. She tossed the seabag onto the elevator floor, the bag responding with a muffled *thunk*. Breathing heavily, she leaned forward against the control panel, then pressed the main lobby button.

* * *

Yanking Ferrante off the floor by his jacket lapels, I connected with a glancing blow to the left side of the wanted criminal's chin. The convicted felon fell backward on top of an end table next to the suite's recliner, smashing it to pieces. I spun and retrieved my gun from underneath the pillow, then turned my head back in Ferrante's direction. *Good . . . he's not moving.*

Dropping to my knees, I attempted to fish the culprit's Beretta from underneath the bed—that's the last thing I remembered before Ferrante smashed me over the back of the head with a leg retrieved from the broken end table.

* * *

Rolling Matt face up with his foot, Ferrante took a step back and removed Joan's Glock from his waistband before aiming it at the center of his forehead. Hearing a quiet knock, he turned and walked in the direction of the door.

"Who is it?"

"Maid service; we've returned to clean the room."

Opening the door a crack, Ferrante barked, "It's late . . . why are you here?"

"There was a do not disturb hanger on the door handle earlier," the maid answered. "As you can see, it's no longer there," she said, glancing at the door handle. "Our records indicate we haven't cleaned the suite today, but we're here now if you . . ."

Ferrante pressed his lips together, shaking his head.

The maid shrugged. "Well, we'll be cleaning the adjacent rooms if you change your—"

"Come back tomorrow," Ferrante snapped, slamming the door shut. He turned around and looked at Matt, still unconscious on the floor. "You don't know how lucky you are, gumshoe." He shoved the Glock back inside his waistband and walked out of the suite and toward the end of the hallway, disappearing down the fire escape stairwell.

* * *

Jostled by her narrow escape, Russo closed her eyes. She steadied herself over the control panel as the elevator began its descent, still breathing heavily and attempting to collect her thoughts.

"Going somewhere?" the passenger behind her asked.

"W . . . what?" Russo mumbled, confused by the question. Opening her eyes, she suddenly realized the passenger in the elevator never exited the floor when she entered, nor was a button pushed for any other floor. "Who the hell is asking?" she demanded in a shrill voice. Pushing herself away from the control panel, she attempted to turn around, only to feel the thunderous jolt of an electric current traverse the length

of her body in less than a millisecond. She dropped unconscious and face down on the elevator floor.

Delia bent over, cuffing the suspect bank robber. "I'll
answer the question for you, Felony. The only place you're
going is to jail."

* * *

Something's not right, Ferrante thought, speed dialing
his top henchman's cell phone repeatedly. Standing on the
ground floor sidewalk just outside the stairwell fire escape exit,
he stuffed the iPhone back into his jacket. Catching a glimpse
of flashing emergency vehicle lights spilling eerily around the
corner of the building, he rushed toward his car. Pointing his
key fob at the driver's side door, he pressed the unlock button.

"Not so fast," he heard a voice in the background yell out.

Wheeling around, Ferrante stood an arm's distance
away from a shadowy figure in the dimly lit resort parking
lot. A snugly fitted fedora-style hat, a buttoned trench coat,
and black leather gloves cast a dark shadow over the identity
of the unexpected visitor. A .38-caliber revolver suddenly
came into view — it was pointed directly at the gang boss.

"Who are you? What do you want?" Ferrante shouted.

"You like to hurt people, don't you?"

"What are you talking about?" Ferrante fired back.

"That's your entire modus operandi, isn't it, Davin?
You're a cruel, vicious, criminal sociopath . . . with a little
sadistic narcissism mixed in for good measure."

"L-look, I don't follow you," the gang leader nervously
replied. "Uh . . . tell you what. I have money . . . it . . . it's in
the trunk," he lied. "Go ahead and take it . . . and we'll both
be on our way. What do you say?" he proposed, a nervous
grin making its way across his face.

No response.

He reached for Joan's Glock tucked in his waistband.

The stranger responded by firing two hollow-point slugs into the convicted felon's upper torso.

Ferrante slid down the side of his Lexus. Multiple trails of blood streaked unevenly down the driver's side door. He slumped over, lying awkwardly against the car between the front and rear wheels. The assailant turned and walked away, disappearing into a darkened field behind the parking lot.

* * *

"What the hell happened?" I asked. Shaking my head, my vision slowly returned. Delia and Agent Morelli stooped down next to me.

"A rhetorical question," Morelli replied. "Once again, Delia was two steps ahead of you," he continued as he and Delia helped me to my feet. "Your assistant handed Joan Russo to us in a neat little package, cuffed and ready to go. We took her and the stolen cash into custody, then rode the elevator with Delia back to the suite number you wrote inside the book of matches handed to her by the bartender. Guess who we discovered with his kisser buried in the carpet?"

I let out a sigh, then rubbed my forehead with my index and middle fingers. "I'm traumatized for life just thinking about you rubbing it in my face whenever we run into each other down the road."

"Looks like Ferrante got the drop on you," Morelli said. "You're damn lucky to be alive . . . always sticking your neck out," he admonished.

"Yeah, he did," I painfully admitted, squinting my eyes and rubbing the back of my head. "Well, what else is new?

We'll just have to—"

"We got him," someone interrupted, a familiar voice.

I turned. "Who said that?"

"I did."

Rubbing my eyes, my visual acuity returned. "Detective Sergeant Kate Blanchard," I yelled out. "What are you doing here?"

"The hotel called MPD after one of their managers was found bound and gagged in his office," she explained. "Delia called the FBI when she couldn't locate you after you left the restaurant with Russo. Rather than wait for Agent Morelli, she rode the elevator to the eleventh floor. Out of sheer coincidence, Russo happened to step inside the elevator with the seabag in hand, obviously attempting to get the hell out of Dodge. Delia recognized Russo and moved to take her down. The hotel staff pointed out the other three thugs after their nonsensical questions at the counter raised red flags."

"Okay . . . and which train to Clarksville was Ferrante attempting to board?" I asked.

"A security guard was making his rounds in a golf cart when he heard the sound of gunfire coming from one of several parking areas, so he went to check it out."

"And?"

"He's dead," Morelli joined in. "The security officer discovered Ferrante on the pavement next to his car."

* * *

"On behalf of my colleagues and our member banks, we cannot thank you enough," the head of the American Bankers Association announced gratefully to Delia and me. Sitting in a row of chairs in front of my desk, John Richardson and his two colleagues beamed in delight knowing the gang's crime spree had come to an end.

"Happy we were able to help," Delia acknowledged, a smile of satisfaction lighting up her face.

The regional vice president of New Corporate Bank raised his hand. "The cash stolen from the most recent robbery has been returned, but what about the money still missing from the other banks they robbed?"

"The FBI and MPD are talking with Russo, her surviving thug colleagues, and their attorneys," I told them. "It might involve a deal of some kind, but it's my understanding most of the cash will be recovered."

Paul Morgan stood, coffee in hand. "Well, what isn't will be covered under what's called a banker's blanket bond," he explained, "which is a policy that protects the bank for losses involving robbery and other covered perils. Our customers have nothing to worry about."

The head of the Western Branch of the Federal Reserve pivoted in his chair. "Did Ms. Russo divulge what she was planning to do . . . or where she was planning to go?"

"Good question, Mr. Metzler," I answered. "Added to the other monies stolen from previous bank jobs, it's believed her plan was to launder most of the cash in unison with country hopping using multiple fake passports. She speaks several languages. It wouldn't have been difficult; the entire planet is awash in these crooks . . . no pun intended."

"Does anyone know who shot and killed Ferrante?" Metzler asked.

Both investigators shook their heads. "That's for the feds and MPD to figure out."

Delia and I shook hands with each of the bank officials, exchanging the normal goodbyes and pleasantries. Closing the door, I turned and locked eyes with my assistant.

Exhaling a quiet breath, I blurted, "I'm glad it's over."

Delia pursed her lips and sighed. "Well, I have news for you . . . it's *not* over."

I turned in her direction, puzzled. "What are you talking about?"

"I'm talking about Ferrante."

"Hold on a moment. He's dead, the money has been recovered, and Russo's in jail along with her cohorts. Checkmate . . . game over."

"Oh, c'mon, Matt. I know you. Neither MPD nor the FBI have a clue as to the identity of his killer. But I know that mind cave of yours, and it either knows or has a pretty good idea who it is. Russo and the gang members have been ruled out, so . . . is it Denny Lovato? He had motive."

"Why would it be him . . . what motive?"

"Because he was infatuated with Joan, not to mention Ferrante threatened his life and gave him a severe beating in that sports bar parking lot."

I nodded. "Okay, he had motive, but not opportunity. He was in the hospital when Ferrante was killed. That rules him out."

"What about—"

"Whoa," I said, shaking my head. "Please . . . stop. You're cherry picking." A pause. "Tell you what . . . remember when you mentioned earlier that you would fill me in regarding the favor you did for your lady friend who works in the jewelry store in the mall? The one who sold the Pandora bracelet and charms to Russo?"

"Uh, yeah," Delia quietly replied, a confused expression appearing as she attempted to recollect their conversation. "I don't get it . . . what does that have to do with Ferrante's murder?"

"Nothing . . . yet, other than you promised to share that

information with me. C'mon, I need something in return for emptying my file," I said, pointing a finger at my temple.

"Uh huh, yeah, okay . . . you mean—"

"Speculation," I interrupted. "Pure speculation . . . a hunch or theory without firm evidence."

"It's still more than what MPD or the FBI knows," she replied in a sarcastic tone.

"Well . . . is it a deal?"

Hesitating, she asked, "Why do I have the feeling you've got something else up your sleeve?"

I cocked an eyebrow. "Why, Delia, to accuse me of ulterior motives just because I'm curious to—"

"Okay, okay, it's a deal," she broke in, "but on one condition."

"And what would that be?" I smirked in anticipation.

"That we discuss *my* favor and *your* speculation over dinner . . . the dinner you promised me earlier."

I pulled a face. "Say, that's right; we never did finish our meal, did we?" I said in a flippant tone, attempting to inject a bit of levity into a conversation that was growing more serious.

"Finished? We never even ordered."

I shook my head and laughed. "Okay, Season's 52 it is," I said, walking in her direction. "Shall we?" I asked, offering my arm.

Delia gave a scornful smile. "You're such a ball-buster."

THE END

THE CASE OF THE NEFARIOUS NEPHEW

—

EPISODE V

PROLOGUE

Framed and wrongfully committed to Paragon State Mental Institution, heiress Melissa Barton authorizes her late father's devoted concierge to retain Private Investigator Matt Duggan. His mission: to uncover and thwart her conspirators' goal of seizing control and plundering the assets of the now rudderless Barton shipping empire. Tag along with Matt Duggan and his loyal assistant Delia Perez as they follow the trail of a sleazy, chiseling attorney, a crooked hospital administrator, and the late Spencer Barton's sinister nephew and soon to be beneficiary of a billion-dollar empire.

PART I

"It's too risky," I objected. "The criminally insane constitute a high percentage of the patients housed in that facility. Your safety cannot be guaranteed, and I don't know if I can help you should something go wrong."

Delia turned in my direction, then made a face. "I'm telling you I can do this," she argued. "I can initiate a self-admission . . . just walk into their ER department and tell them I'm harboring suicidal thoughts. Once admitted, I can, with a bit of stealth, locate Melissa, let her know what's going on, and that we'll both be out of there as quickly as I can get word back to you."

I sighed again, shaking my head. "Still, things can go wrong . . . and very quickly. Paragon Mental Asylum is a state-run maximum security forensic psychiatric hospital . . . notorious for housing deranged criminals. Even the name Paragon sounds out of joint. That's a word better suited for use with a new-generation computer featuring artificial intelligence or neural network pattern recognition abilities, not a facility for the criminally insane."

The prospective client glanced at Delia, nodding in agreement. "Matt is correct. I understand what I am suggesting is risky," he said. Leaning back in a chair opposite my battered desk, J. Everett Holland sat with his legs crossed. Parked next to Delia, the six-foot-tall sixty-some-thing-year-old man displayed distinguished but chiseled good looks. His gunmetal gray hair complemented a pair of tired, galaxy blue eyes. Wearing a crisp gray business suit, a white shirt with a matching blue-and-white striped tie, the former personal assistant to the late shipping magnate Spencer Barton held tight to what appeared to be a red-colored two-inch expansion folder.

I exhaled a deep sigh and gave a harried look at Holland. "Should Delia be discovered, it could be really bad news . . . for her. It's a no-brainer to say that what you want Delia to do really bothers me . . . and that's an understatement."

Holland nodded. "I never argue with someone I agree with, but it's the quickest way of locating Melissa and telling us exactly where inside the facility she's being held."

"And that's only if she's successful—and that's a big if," I added.

Everett Holland pushed his chair away from my desk, shaking his head in frustration. "Please allow me to restate why I'm here," he began, his tone of voice abrupt. "Spencer Barton's adult daughter Melissa has been wrong-fully committed to Paragon upon petition by Mr. Barton's nephew, Ray Sutton. It's believed Mr. Sutton coerced or paid a mental health worker who was treating Melissa for depression to file a petition with the court in cahoots with Paragon's chief medical superintendent and their paid-for attorney."

"A court order to involuntarily commit Melissa for depression?" Delia asked, a perplexed look on her face.

"After falsely accusing her of being suicidal . . . yes, that is correct," Everett continued. "Melissa is the sole surviving heiress of Spencer Barton's personal fortune, known to be in the billions. And it's my further belief that his greedy, no-account nephew has plans to have her declared mentally incompetent. That would place him next in line to inherit the estate, ahead of Melissa. There are no other surviving family or relatives."

"Did Spencer Barton have a will? Was there a trust of any kind?" I asked.

Everett shook his head. "Oddly enough, that's a no to both questions . . . and no one knows why. He died intestate. As the only surviving child, the intestacy statutes give everything to his only child Melissa . . . his personal fortune, property, the shipping business . . . everything."

"You mean unless she's locked up in a mental institution, and/or declared incompetent," I asserted.

"Correct."

"Has Melissa retained legal counsel?"

"With my assistance . . . yes, she has," Everett answered, swiveling in his chair and crossing his legs. "And it was her idea to retain your services," he added.

"Her? Who is this attorney?"

"Her name is Erin Lauber, a sole practitioner. She's in court today on an unrelated matter."

"Hmm. I know a lot of attorneys, but I'm not familiar with this particular counselor. Are you telling me she's on board with this idea?"

"Totally."

"Has the attorney done anything on Melissa's behalf?" Delia chimed in.

"Attorney Lauber is preparing to initiate appropriate legal proceedings to challenge the court-ordered involuntary commitment," he answered. "But you can rest assured the hospital's current chief administrator, along with their 'anything can be proven by two false witnesses' pettifogger, will do everything they can to thwart those efforts."

"Pettifogger? I haven't heard that crooked attorney description in a while," I chuckled, "but I agree. That could or will allow those parties to stonewall long enough to have her declared mentally incompetent . . . and indefinitely committed."

"That's exactly what Melissa's attorney and I believe their end game to be," Holland speculated.

I turned and exchanged glances with Delia, worried. "Del, you know I have the utmost confidence in you, but there have to be additional safeguards," I insisted.

"Okay," she replied in a jocular tone. "So, who or what do you have in mind?"

"Blanchard and Morelli," I immediately answered.

Delia bobbed her head and smiled. "Good answer."

"Blanchard and Morelli?" Holland repeated with a curious look.

"They're my primary contacts with MPD and the FBI. I want people I know and trust who I can count on to act at a moment's notice to extricate Delia out of that hellscape should the need arise."

"I'm not familiar with either party, but it makes sense to me."

Delia glanced at Holland. "Now you know why I work with this man."

I smiled, then turned and locked eyes with Holland. "One last thing: What's in this for you?"

Holland took in a deep breath. "Fair question, Mr. Duggan."

"Please . . . call me Matt."

"All right, Matt," he said, sporting a half-smile. "I worked for Spencer Barton for more than thirty years. He was a good man, a fair and honest man, and generous to a fault. I did everything he asked and expected of me," he explained. "Even though he's no longer with us, he still wouldn't expect anything less of me . . . and that includes what's happening to his daughter."

Acknowledging with a repetitive nod, I pushed my chair away from my desk and stood. "Because Melissa is represented by legal counsel, I'll need to speak with her attorney before I can greenlight this."

"I'll make the arrangements," Holland said, standing and gently tossing the file he had held tightly onto my desk. "Be at Lauber's office tomorrow morning at ten." He looked down at the folder. "I'll need you to bring that with you when you meet with her." He stood there, remaining silent.

I cast a curious glance at the binder, then reached out and grabbed the thick file, pulling it toward me before glancing up and locking eyes with the middle-age concierge. A pause ensued. "All right . . . I give up. What's inside?"

Holland grimaced. "A lot of unfortunate souls' worst nightmares."

PART II

"Damn . . . this is mind-boggling," I blurted in disbelief.

Standing next to a portable table used to examine and organize numerous documents related to pending cases, Delia nodded in agreement. "Holland was right. It wouldn't be a stretch or hyperbole to describe the contents of the binder he threw on your desk as a Pandora's box of nightmares . . . particularly if they're true."

"For sure," I quietly mumbled. "A conglomeration of greed, corruption, and evil . . . right here in front of us. I cannot begin to imagine what's going on inside that so-called snake pit of a mental hospital."

Delia shook her head in disgust. "Counseling after my husband's death helped me a great deal. Melissa and the other illicitly admitted Paragon patients are being cruelly exploited under the guise of mental health treatment." She turned and gave me a determined look. "We need to do something, Matt."

I returned Delia's gaze along with a supportive nod. "Holland asked me to bring this folder when we meet with Melissa's attorney. Now I understand why."

"All of which begs the question of how or where Holland obtained these documents," Delia said.

"My thoughts exactly, and one you can rest assured

Attorney Lauber will be asked when we meet with her tomorrow."

* * *

Law Office of Erin Lauber, Esq.

"Please have a seat," Attorney Lauber graciously offered after introductions, escorting Delia and me into her private office.

"Would you care for coffee, tea, or some other beverage?" she asked.

"No, thank you," I said.

"I'm good," Delia echoed.

Smiling softly, she sat behind her desk. She switched her computer monitor off, pushed it to the side, then moved a large file to a credenza behind her. Lauber pressed the intercom button on her desk phone.

"Receptionist."

"This is Erin. Hold my calls."

"Yes, ma'am."

A very attractive natural blonde, Erin Lauber, wore a braided bun with multiple weaved strands on top and a twirled bun at the nape. She had light makeup that highlighted her features. She exuded an air of confidence and professionalism, wearing a simple navy blue suit with heels and a white blouse. Her jewelry was simple and tasteful.

After engaging in several minutes of informal small talk, it was time to get down to business. "Delia and I are here on behalf of your client, Melissa Barton, subsequent to a visit yesterday by J. Everett Holland, the late Spencer Barton's personal assistant," I explained.

"Yes, it's my understanding that he briefed you

regarding the situation involving Melissa's involuntary commitment to Paragon State Hospital," Lauber confirmed.

"He did."

Delia exchanged looks with the attorney. "What have you done to get her released?" she asked bluntly, not mincing words.

Lauber craned her head and gazed at Delia. "First of all, you just don't waltz into a state-run mental hospital or a court and demand a patient's release following a commitment order from a judge, Ms. Perez," Melissa's attorney explained in a prickly tone.

I raised my hands. "Whoa . . ." I said, making the time-out gesture. "Everett explained that you were in the process of initiating legal proceedings. We just want to know what you've done to secure her release before we discuss with you what we have in mind should your efforts be delayed . . . or denied."

My assistant pushed her chair back slightly and crossed her legs. "Oh, and please call me Delia," she added, a slight smirk appearing.

Attorney Lauber uttered a weary sigh, then placed her hands on her desk. "Before we go any further, let's agree to address one another on a first-name basis," she suggested, a pleasant smile returning. "Then I'll provide you with a quick summary of events leading up to Melissa's involuntary admission."

"We're all ears," I said.

Attorney Lauber stood and paced the room. "Melissa has been treated for depression and anxiety since she was a teenager. While it may seem odd, this is a common affliction among children from affluent families. The pressure to succeed, excel in school, be model children, and so on. And being an only child can exacerbate the problem."

I nodded. "I've read and heard about it."

Attorney Lauber continued to pace. "Melissa had no siblings she could lean on or relate to. Adding to that, her mother died when she was eleven. Her father did his best to be there for her, but running a business the size of Barton Shipping placed a huge demand on his time."

"So . . . what happened?" Delia asked.

"When Melissa turned eighteen, her father began the process of grooming her to take over the business. At some point, the pressure became too much, and she suffered a nervous breakdown. He sought treatment for his daughter once again, and that's when Barton's estranged nephew suddenly crawled out of the woodwork."

I raised a hand. "Okay, so who is this so-called nephew, and what exactly is his involvement?"

"I'm getting to that." Lauber returned to her chair and sat. "Shortly thereafter," she continued, "Spencer Barton died—a massive stroke, according to Everett."

Delia gave a sympathetic look. "You don't have to be a shrink to know that the cumulative effect of all those events exacerbated Melissa's illness. An only child feeling the pressure to outshine, then her mother dies when she's eleven, followed by a diagnosis of depression as a teen, accompanied by a nervous breakdown as her father begins grooming her to take over the business . . . And if that isn't or wasn't enough, her father and only surviving immediate family member dies unexpectedly. That's more personal tragedy than the strongest person should have to deal with."

Processing Delia's summary of events, I paused before shifting in my chair. I exchanged a glance with Lauber. "Please continue."

Erin pushed her chair back slightly. "That's when Holland stepped in and assumed the role of surrogate father.

He personally handled Mr. Spencer's funeral arrangements and worked very closely with Melissa to run the shipping business, balancing those duties with the outpatient mental health treatment she needed."

"How did that work out?"

"According to Everett, it was working well—that is, until Ray Sutton cooked up plans with the current chief hospital administrator, a psychiatrist by the name of Jacob Lundsten. Sutton had previously worked for the hospital as an orderly. He used his knowledge of the system in cahoots with his new partner-in-crime Lundsten, and their bunco attorney Marvin Shyner to Baker Act Melissa after falsely reporting she was expressing suicidal ideations during therapy with her mental health counselor."

"Did I hear you say Marvin Shyner?"

"Yes, more widely known in and outside the legal community as Marvin Shyster," Lauren replied. "Have you heard of him?"

"Yeah, I've heard of the crook," I answered in a disparaging tone. "Word has it the state bar court judge has been after him for permanent disbarment following repeated suspensions."

Delia uncrossed her legs and leaned forward. "Hold on . . . let's back up a bit. My understanding of the law is that a person cannot be held for involuntary psychiatric examination longer than seventy-two hours . . . is that correct?"

Attorney Lauber nodded. "Correct, that's the law. However, Sutton and his two confidence men were able to convince a judge that it was in Melissa's best interests for her three-day involuntary admission to be extended."

"Allowing the time needed to document her stay with falsified medical records and reports recommending permanent institutionalization," I interjected.

Delia leaned back in her chair and crossed her legs again. "You said something about Sutton working previously for the hospital as an orderly. Can you elaborate more on that?"

"He was fired by the former administrator, Milton O'Toole, for assault, stealing from patients and shaking down family members," Erin explained. "He was subsequently arrested, and with help from his wannabe consigliere, they cut a deal with the prosecutor for probation and time served."

"Have you had any contact with Dr. O'Toole?" Delia inquired.

"No."

"Why not?" I asked, perplexed.

"You must not have gone through all the papers that are in the folder Everett left with you," Lauber replied, pointing at the file. "He's locked up in his own hospital."

"What? Explain that to me."

"We didn't go through every single document," Delia chimed in. "The first thing we noticed was an envelope attached to the inside of the folder; there's an undated, unsigned, handwritten note inside stating that the enclosed admission records are of patients involuntarily committed, none of whom met the requirements for forced admission."

"That's correct," Lauber acknowledged with a confirming nod before responding to my bid for an explanation. "O'Toole was taken into custody by MPD two weeks ago. A security guard called 911 after noticing an adult male running around a well-publicized car dealership at approximately two in the morning, naked as a jaybird, howling and covered in mud and debris following a severe rainstorm. He wouldn't comply with the responding officers' orders, so they tased him and took him into custody. He was still incoherent and delusional twenty-four hours later, so he was Baker Acted. No one has any idea what happened or what caused this reputable physician and former hospital administrator to go off his rocker."

I sighed. "Don't tell me . . . he's still there?"

"Along with Melissa and more than a dozen other fraudulent admissions per that folder you're holding," Lauber divulged.

"Which begs another question: How was Holland able to get possession of these documents?" I asked, glancing at the red expansion file before looking back at Lauber.

"I don't know," she replied. "He wouldn't disclose where or how he obtained it. But he did tell me Sutton knows he has it and has threatened to kill Melissa if it's turned over to the authorities."

I took a deep breath, then turned and locked eyes with my assistant. "You still good with this?"

Delia pursed her lips, then let out an angry sigh. "Damn right I am . . . Let's do it."

PART III

"What's the status on Paris Hilton?"

Dr. Lundsten returned an irritated look at Ray Sutton. "Same as the last status I provided. She's confined to a private room, alert and oriented, but tranquil after administering midazolam . . . not that you would know what that is."

Sutton wore an unpleasant smirk. "I know it's a central nervous system depressant . . . or I suppose you've forgotten how long I worked here, Doctor Jekyll. I've seen your loonies booted numerous times with all kinds of drugs . . . even assisted your staff in doing so on occasion. And knock off the smart-ass remarks every time I ask you a question about our Princess of Bel Air."

"You're a vulgar son-of-a-bitch, Sutton," Lundsten snapped. "We don't boot medications here. That's what hopheads on the streets do . . . like you."

Sutton stormed in a threatening manner toward the newly appointed hospital director. "You know, Doc, one of these days you're going to open that smart mouth of yours one time too . . ."

The door to Lundsten's office swung open, and a familiar face entered the room.

Sutton spun around. "Well, well, look who the cat

dragged in. It's our Perry Mason wannabe," he voiced sarcastically, a smug expression crossing his face. He turned around again and returned to Lundsten's desk, pulling out a guest chair and sitting down. Leaning back and crossing his legs, with his ankle resting on his knee, Sutton adjusted his pants leg so the crease would fall properly. "So, counselor, what brings you here to Looney Town today?"

Marvin Shyner appeared to be about forty years old, with sharp eyes, a thin mouth, and a face resembling a bulldog. He was dressed in a dark blue suit, a light blue dress shirt, and a slim navy-blue tie that looked almost out of style.

"Is there something you want to tell us, counselor?" Sutton prodded.

Shyner placed his briefcase on the floor next to Lundsten's desk. "Yeah. I just left court about an hour ago," he announced wearily. "Our patient is now being represented by Erin Lauber. She has filed a notice of appearance on behalf of Melissa Barton."

"It's probably Holland's doing," Lundsten speculated.

"She's no pushover . . . that much I can tell you."

Sutton jumped out of his chair. "Hold on," he yelled out, exchanging glances with Lundsten and Shyner. "Why should that be a surprise? Did either of you believe for a second that Lauber or some other attorney wouldn't challenge the commitment order?" He turned and faced Shyner. "Is there anything else you want to tell me, counselor?"

The portly attorney walked up to Sutton. "Yeah . . . as a matter of fact, I do. Why don't you go piss up a rope."

* * *

"Well, it's official," I said to Delia as we drove back to the agency. "I'll schedule a conference call with Blanchard and Morelli as soon as we get back to the office. It's time to bring them into the loop."

Delia nodded. "And let's arrange an in-house meeting with Lauber. She can update both of them from a legal perspective, including any need for court orders and warrants."

I let out a deep sigh. "I'm still concerned about your safety, Del. You won't be allowed to have a cell phone or access any landline. You can't wear a wire or bring in a tracking device of any kind. They would find that on you within minutes when you change into hospital garb."

"So, we focus on what we can do," Delia said. "And the first thing will be to hack into their computer system."

"Which means we'll need a warrant."

"Correct."

I slowed my car and flipped on the turn signal. "According to Lauber, Melissa's forced admission, along with the damning documentation in the folder, should be sufficient to obtain any necessary warrants." I turned into my agency's parking lot and parked in my private office space. I craned my head and looked at my assistant. "What's your plan for spoofing their computer?"

Delia shifted in her seat. "The FBI forensics lab will need to provide a copy of a tainted or malware software update . . . a Trojan horse of sorts. Morelli can make those arrangements. When it's received, I can execute the update from my computer to theirs, making it appear as if it's from a trusted source and related to their personal business model. I'll obtain Lundsten's email address at Paragon and forward it directly to him. Once he opens it, we'll have a foothold into their system."

"I get it . . . then you can download Melissa's falsified medical records and any other incriminating documents and forward those to Lauber and Morelli before your admission. Neither Lundsten nor anyone else in the facility will be any the wiser."

"Bingo," Delia said. "Once admitted, it's my intention to locate a landline or loose cellphone and contact you as soon as I've confirmed Melissa's whereabouts."

"Roger that. Rest assured, though—Morelli, Blanchard, and I will be close by in a surveillance van. And just so you know . . . under no circumstances are you to remain in Paragon longer than twenty-four hours. After that, we'll be entering the facility on a separate warrant to remove you and Melissa, whether we've heard from you or not."

Noticing my anxious look, Delia gave a reassuring smile.

"I'm not worried . . . not one bit. I know you've got my back."

PART IV

Arriving at FBI headquarters later that morning, Delia and I strolled into the decades-old rectangular-shaped federal building. Built of buff limestone and granite, the architectural style of planar surfaces and ornamentation gave rise to a distinguished look. After showing my PI license and badge, I relinquished my revolver to a senior member of the security staff. We were scanned using handheld metal detector wands followed by a full video body scan. Handed chip-embedded guest badges, Delia and I were escorted to a sizable conference room on the third floor where Blanchard, Lauber, Morelli, and FBI legal counsel Bryan Grissinger engaged in small talk as they sat around the conference table waiting for the remaining two participants. A continental breakfast cuisine consisting of light pastries, fruit, coffee, and juice was available on a built-in counter. Folders, writing pads, and pens were provided and strategically placed around the table, its size adjusted to fit the six participants. The red expandable file I left earlier with Lauber was visible next to her writing pad.

"Well, it appears Inspector Clouseau has just honored us with his presence," Morelli teased.

"Very funny," I fired back, taking a seat. "By the way, I just heard you recently qualified as the best marksman among your fellow agents."

Morelli stopped smiling. "What are you talking about?"

"Yeah, for real," I said. "Someone told me he asked you about it the other day, and you said, 'Nothing to it. I shoot first and draw the circles afterward.'"

The room erupted in laughter.

Morelli chuckled. "Okay, okay . . . Everyone's present, so let's get on with it. Place all cell phones on silent mode." He glanced at me. "You have the floor."

I cast a thoughtful glance around the room. "Thank you, Agent Morelli. Everyone knows who's who and why we're here. Melissa Barton's attorney, Erin Lauber, will begin the briefing. Please give her your undivided attention," I requested, turning my head in her direction.

Pushing her chair back and standing, Lauber launched into a lengthy statement regarding her client, much like the opening remarks in a jury trial. Confining her assertions to the facts backed by documentation obtained from Paragon, she outlined her client's history, including the allegation that at least a dozen other patients were knowingly and wrongfully admitted to the notorious state-run lunatic asylum.

Morelli glanced at the red accordion file, then looked up at Lauber. "Who provided this documentation?" he asked.

"A confidential informant whose identity I am not at liberty to reveal," she replied.

Morelli sighed and pursed his lips. "I must respectfully remind legal counsel that any non-law enforcement person who provides information may be required to testify in court. That's right out of—"

"Hold on a minute," the bureau's legal counsel interrupted, dropping a handful of documents from the red file he was reviewing onto the table. Wearing a pin-striped three-button navy suit, a white dress shirt, and a matching blue tie, the middle-aged attorney with slicked-back hair and a thin nose leaned back in his swivel chair. "You're correct," he continued. "The informant may ultimately be required to testify; we'll cross that bridge later." He turned and looked at Lauber. "What we have here, on its surface, appears to meet the probable cause requirements that a crime has been committed, although it could be argued it's hearsay."

"So, what you're saying is—"

Grissinger raised his hand. "What I'm saying is the prosecutorial review of all the evidence will determine whether we can mount a successful prosecution in court." He paused. "Plainly and legally speaking . . . we need more."

"We presumed you would make that a requirement," Attorney Lauber acknowledged, "so I'll hand this discussion back to Private Investigator Matt Duggan and his assistant, Delia Perez. They'll explain their proposal for obtaining the corroborating documentation." She sat and craned her head back in my direction. "Mr. Duggan."

Delia and I shared the floor while explaining our proposal to hack into Paragon's computers, followed by Delia's admission into the hospital by faking suicidal ideation. "It's Delia's suggestion that we obtain what we believe will be matching, falsified medical records and documentation; in other words, exact duplicates of the documents that are on the table and in the red expansion file next to Ms. Lauber."

"Corroborating evidence 101," Delia added.

The legal counsel for the FBI nodded. "Exactly . . . solid, factual evidence. It's what we'll need for another warrant to enter Paragon and remove those patients, arrest our three principal reprobates, Lundsten, Shyner, and Sutton, and confiscate the hospital's computers and other records."

Lauber stood again. "With the approval of the bureau,

and assuming a warrant to hack Paragon's computer system is issued, I will arrange a follow-up meeting with FBI legal counsel after Delia and Matt obtain the matching documentation. We'll review and authenticate the evidence collected. If we're in agreement at that meeting, we'll seek to obtain the additional court orders and arrest warrants needed."

Morelli turned and whispered to Grissinger, "Let's get the ball rolling with what we have and obtain the necessary warrant to hack into Paragon's computer system. I'll make arrangements for Matt and Delia to work with our digital forensics people regarding the malware needed."

Continuing his review of the documents in Lauber's red file, the FBI legal counsel motioned his consent with a thumbs-up.

"It's a go," Morelli turned around and shouted.

Grissinger raised an eyebrow. "Bear in mind that we need to gather enough evidence to prove Lundsten, Shyner, and Sutton are part of a conspiracy. The more we gather, the tighter their noose becomes. Keep that in mind."

Morelli looked at Delia and me. "You heard what the man said."

"Understood," came the reply.

Blanchard pushed her seat back and stood. "MPD will take responsibility for coordinating a joint MPD and FBI command post on the day Delia is admitted . . . assuming she is convincing enough for Paragon to admit her."

Delia grinned. "Trust me, I'll be admitted."

"Our three perps may or may not be inside the facility when we make our descent onto Paragon," I jumped in. "We'll need to know their whereabouts and take them into custody in unison with the raid. It's likely they'll flee if they get word, so let's get them behind bars before they have a chance to hightail it out of Dodge."

"I concur," Blanchard piped in. "We'll work with Matt and Delia to pinpoint their location . . . when the time is right."

Delia pointed at the red accordion file on the table. "We should arrange for independent physical and psychological examinations for Melissa and every person documented in that folder."

Lauber gave a confirming nod. "From a legal and medical standpoint, it would be the smart thing to do. A comparison of the authentic IMEs to the fabricated documents should seal the fate of the gang of three."

Morelli stood and glanced around the room. "If there are no further comments or questions, this meeting is concluded."

Entering the passcode and unmuting her iPhone, Lauber noticed a text message from her office imploring her to call immediately. Walking to a corner of the conference room, she called her receptionist, alternating for several minutes between listening and responding in a hurried, but hushed tone.

"Everything okay?" I asked.

Lowering her cell phone, she turned and locked eyes with me. "It's Holland," she replied, a grim expression appearing. "He's disappeared."

PART V

"Have you lost your mind?" Lundsten berated Sutton. The unscrupulous physician and hospital administrator turned and continued his visual examination of Holland as he lay unconscious on a gurney in the morgue section of the hospital basement.

Sutton gave a sarcastic laugh. "Lost minds are your business, Doctor. Arranging for people to get lost is mine," he sneered, returning a sinister glance. He whirled around and gazed at the drugged concierge. "Don't worry, nothing will happen to our interloper here until he provides more information regarding what he knows about efforts to secure Melissa's release. I know he talked to the cops, and he's going to tell us exactly what he told them . . . and you're going to help."

"Help you? Help you with what?"

"Does the hospital have a supply of sodium amytal or sodium pentothal?"

Lundsten gave Sutton a sideways glance. "What do you have in mind?" he asked, a suspicious look appearing on his face.

"You're a smart man, Doc . . . What do you think?"

Lundsten took a deep breath. "Truth serum is a myth, Sutton. Research has proven those drugs are unreliable when used for that purpose. There is currently no drug proven to cause consistent or predictable truth-telling. That's a Hollywood fantasy."

"Call it what you want, but we're going to use it if he doesn't tell us what he knows."

"Those drugs are for therapeutic use only," Lundsten insisted. "They can be dangerous if used as a truth drug to force confessions or other information out of patients."

Sutton pressed his lips together. "Like I said, if Holland doesn't cooperate, you're going to help me administer whatever you have—do you understand?"

Lundsten remained silent. He walked over to the unconscious Holland and checked his respiration and pulse again, while Sutton opened a hospital garment locker. Removing his shirt and slacks, he donned the standard white garb of a hospital orderly. He clipped on a photo ID dating back to his previous employment with the hospital.

"What are you up to?" Lundsten asked.

"Stay here with Holland," he ordered. "I'll be back shortly."

* * *

"What do you mean, Holland's disappeared?" I asked. The others in the conference room stopped what they were doing. They turned and looked in Lauber's direction.

"Holland was supposed to drop by the office before noon today. He told my greeter earlier he planned to drop off a garment and shoe bag for Melissa along with a makeup kit in anticipation of her being extricated from Paragon," Lauber explained. "Thirty minutes after he failed to show up, my receptionist began attempts to contact him, with no response. That's when she called and left a message on my voicemail. That was an hour ago. I've called his cell phone several times. It goes straight to voicemail."

"I'll issue a BOLO on behalf of MPD," Blanchard said.

I whirled around and stared at Morelli. "Looks like Delia and I will have to take a rain check on the malware. We've got a missing concierge to locate." We started to leave.

"Hold on," Morelli blurted out. He glanced at Blanchard before pivoting back to me. "That's our job. You stay out of it until you hear back from me or Blanchard. Is that clear?"

I gave a rascally grin. "Anything you say, chief."

Morelli winced. "Wait a minute." He turned and glanced at Blanchard. "She's the . . . I'm the . . . Hey, are you fucking with me, Duggan?"

"Never," I said, my smile widening.

Giving me a stern look, the senior FBI agent picked up the landline and dialed his administrative assistant. "Beth, bring me the dossiers on Sutton, Lundsten, and Shyner." He dropped the handset back on its cradle and glanced at Delia and me. "Go to computer forensics and let them know what you need. After that, carry on with your usual tasks until I contact you about the hacking warrant. And don't go searching for Holland. Clear?" A forced smile followed. "Oh, and one more thing . . . if for any reason I do need your help, don't—"

I chuckled. "Yeah, yeah, I know," I interrupted. "Don't stick my neck out."

Morelli nodded. "Took the words right out of the unpleasant taste in my mouth," he muttered, his irritation palpable.

* * *

"You'd better come over here," Lundsten whispered, speaking in a hushed tone on his cell phone.

Shyner made a face. "Why? Is . . . ?"

"It's Sutton," came the curt reply. "He's kidnapped and drugged Holland. He has him restrained here in the hospital's morgue, and he's threatening to use barbiturates to extract information about Melissa Barton."

"The damn fool." Shyner scowled. "He's going to screw up this entire operation." He took a deep breath. "Play along until I arrive."

"You'd better hurry. He just left, but said he'd be back. He's up to something."

* * *

Driving back to the office, Delia fidgeted in her seat. "You really enjoy breaking Morelli's balls, don't you?"

I laughed. "He'll get over it . . . he always does."

"Morelli and Blanchard are your most frequent contacts for all our cases," she reminded me. "It's probably not wise to—"

"To do what?" I interrupted.

"Like what I know you're going to do," she fired back, "which is go after and find Holland, even after Morelli told you to back off."

I laughed again. "He told us to carry on with our regular tasks until we hear from him about the warrant . . . and that's exactly what we're going to do."

"Matt, you really should—"

"I have a good working relationship with Morelli and Blanchard," I interjected again. "Keep in mind that they often come to us for information on criminals they're investigating . . . information that only you and I know or can provide. They need us as much as we need them."

Delia took a deep breath. She knew I wouldn't wait for either Blanchard or Morelli.

"And I'm sure you noticed Morelli had no intention of sharing any information on those perps in those dossiers."

"Yeah, I caught that."

"We'll use search engines on the internet to find the last known residential addresses of our three culprits based on what we know. Then we'll set up surveillance, starting with Sutton. We both know he's the key to this whole operation."

"No argument there."

"Once we have him in our sights, we'll be on him like a duck on a June bug. My instinct tells me he'll lead us straight to Holland."

"And your intuition is usually correct."

"If we confirm that the gang of three are involved and/ or have assisted in the illegal detention of this man, then hacking Paragon's computer system becomes irrelevant."

Delia turned and smiled knowingly. "Checkmate."

PART VI

The activation switch was triggered, and the double doors of the hospital basement slowly opened. As Lundsten caught sight of a wheelchair making its way inside, his first observation was of several IV bags attached to an IV pole. The chair was occupied by a patient covered with both a sheet and blanket. Sutton was behind the chair, pushing it through and into the makeshift morgue.

Son-of-a-bitch . . . that must be the Barton girl. What the hell is he planning to do with her? The hospital administrator stepped away from the unconscious Holland and walked briskly toward Sutton and the occupied wheelchair. He pulled the bedding down and away from the face of the covered patient. "Just as I thought," he mumbled, disgusted.

"What did you say, Doc? I didn't catch that," Sutton asked mockingly.

"What is she doing here?"

"I'll explain it to you in a minute, Doc."

Lundsten was furious. "She's sedated. You don't push a sedated patient around in a wheelchair."

"Says who?" Sutton barked.

"According to hospital regulations, you idiot."

A sarcastic laugh followed. "She's strapped in, Doctor Jekyll. Our leading lady isn't going anywhere."

"You didn't answer my question. Why did you bring her down here?"

Before Sutton could answer, the basement double doors opened again. A short, burly figure with a waddling gait resembling that of a penguin ambled into the basement. He wore a three-piece light brown pinstriped suit, and his matching brown wingtips were barely noticeable underneath the ill-fitting trousers, with the leg openings dragging on the floor with every step.

"Well, if it isn't Atticus Finch in the flesh," Sutton sarcastically commented, unbuttoning and removing his white orderly jacket.

Greeting his partner-in-crime with a look of contempt, the corpulent Shyner retorted with an angry barrage. "Shut up, Sutton," he fired back. "Atticus Finch wouldn't give a dried-up piece of snot like you the time of day."

Hurrying around the chair with a furious look, Sutton threw the jacket onto the basement floor.

"Knock it off . . . both of you," Lundsten shouted.

Wheezing with every breath, the unscrupulous attorney glanced back and forth between the Barton girl and Holland. "We all agreed on how this was supposed to work. And now it's gone completely off the rails. Why are these two here?" he demanded.

Sutton jumped off the corner of the desk where he had been sitting. "I'll tell both of you clowns why they're down here. Because I have firsthand knowledge that Holland has been in touch with the cops, and I intend to find out why. To ensure a more successful outcome, both he and my cousin, the queen bee, will be moved to a more secure location. The good news is that the three of us don't know anything about Holland's disappearance. There's no evidence linking any of us to him."

"And what about the Barton girl, genius?" Shyner said. "If the authorities come here with a warrant, how will we explain her absence?"

Sutton walked over and stood next to Melissa, still slumped and sedated in the wheelchair. "We'll tell them the princess escaped. Right before we leave with these two, we'll report her as an escapee. That will give me time to sweat them both at an empty warehouse before we return her to the hospital. Then we can report that she returned on her own, just walked herself back inside like nothing happened. It will support our claim to keep her here permanently."

"And what about Holland?" Lundsten asked.

Sutton chuckled. "He'll be taking a long nap with the fishes. Like I said earlier, no one can connect him to us, and he won't be around later to say otherwise."

"That's murder," Shyner reminded him. "We all agreed that option was off the table."

"Oh, so you actually do know something about the law," Sutton said with a sneer. "Brilliant legal deduction on your part, Matlock. Well, guess what? It's back on the table."

"This has gone too far," Lundsten interjected. "If murder is part of this scheme, I want nothing further to do with it . . . do you hear me?"

Sutton snorted a scornful laugh. "Yeah, I heard you . . . loud and clear." Walking up to Lundsten, he slugged the hospital administrator in the face, knocking him to the floor. "Now you've heard me," he thundered, standing over the unconscious doctor sprawled on the cold concrete.

Startled by Sutton's attack on Lundsten, Shyner grabbed him by the arm and pulled him away. "There's no need for this," he implored. "We all need to take a moment and think about what we're doing."

Sutton spun around. "That's an excellent suggestion,

counselor," he replied with an angry snarl. "Sometimes you actually do give good advice." He paused. "So, that's what I just did, and now I'm telling you and Doctor Jekyll here that I'm in charge of this operation from now on. What I say goes . . . understand?"

Blood trickled down the corner of Lundsten's mouth. Dazed, he placed a hand against the left side of his face, which was now red and swollen from the blow.

"For Christ's sake, help me get him on his feet," Shyner implored, struggling to stoop down and assist the semiconscious doctor in standing up off the basement floor.

"Get up and get those drugs I asked about earlier," Sutton shouted, ignoring Shyner. "And bring half a dozen syringes. Be back in fifteen minutes."

PART VII

"Whoa, take a look at this," Delia called out, pointing to the address on the office desktop. "This is Sutton's last known residential address per the new location software I installed a few months ago."

"I see it." I took a step back. "Hmm, imagine that."

Delia turned her head. "Yeah, really . . . what a coincidence," she uttered in a cynical tone. "That address is only a few miles from the Barton Shipping main offices."

I acknowledged with a nod. "Along with a group of warehouses used as a primary distribution center, located on the opposite side and down the road a mile or so."

Delia pushed her chair back and stood. "Are you considering that he might—"

"I believe the cliché is . . . are you thinking what I'm thinking?" I cut in.

Delia made a cynical face before continuing, "Be using an empty Barton Shipping depot to warehouse a kidnapped Holland?"

I pressed my lips together and bobbed my head.

"Then you and I are tuned in to the same pondering channel."

Smiling, I said, "Let's gather what we need and set up surveillance on Sutton. Go ahead and upload his residential address into your iPhone and confirm the route."

Delia tapped in the information, hit enter, waited a moment, then looked at me. "We're good."

* * *

"Hurry up," Sutton shouted, standing behind Lundsten and Shyner, both pushing wheelchairs containing their abducted captives through a warehouse side door and into the darkened storage facility after removing them from an unmarked hospital wheelchair van.

"I can't see a damn thing," Shyner complained, unable to navigate the musty darkness.

"Hold on," Sutton replied, taking the lead and lighting the way using his cell phone as a flashlight. "There's a vacant office about fifty feet ahead on the left. Follow me inside with these two," he directed, nodding at Melissa and Holland. "C'mon, you schmucks," he bellowed. "Get them inside and flip the light switch by the door."

"Then what?" Shyner asked.

"We wait until they wake up." Sutton grabbed Lundsten by the shirt collar and shoved him toward Melissa and Holland. "Prop them up as best you can in those chairs," he ordered. Lighting a cigarette, he took a long drag before turning and blowing the smoke in Shyner's face. "I'm getting tired of waiting for miss prissy and her chauffeur to finish their nap."

"Talk to Lundsten—that's above my pay grade."

"So is being a lawyer," Sutton retorted.

Lundsten turned around. "It could be hours before they're fully conscious," he said in a muffled tone, his jaw still throbbing from the earlier blow to the face.

Sutton opened a medical bag that he had brought from

the hospital. He reached inside and grabbed several vials of sodium amytal and syringes that his partner-in-crime had been forced to bring. He laid them out on a desk in the abandoned office.

"This is a mistake," Lundsten pleaded. "What you're planning to do could kill them. Even when they come around, they'll be groggy and confused, with residual amounts of the previous sedative in their system. Using that drug could prove fatal."

Sutton growled menacingly at Lundsten. "Shut up, Doc, unless you want the right side of your face to match the left side."

"Everyone settle down," Shyner hollered, fighting the urge to yawn. "It's three in the morning," he pointed out, tapping his watch. "All I can say is that something better happen . . . and soon. By the time they wake up, the three of us will be asleep."

Sutton gave an angry kick to the side of the desk. A moment later, he wheeled around, a sinister grin appearing. "Hold on a minute," he mused, snapping his fingers. "I'm going back to my apartment. I have something there that I believe will counter their sedation. I'll be back in twenty minutes."

* * *

Driving along the metro thoroughfare toward the western side of the city, I gave Delia a sideways glance. "What's your GPS telling you regarding the time of arrival to Sutton's address?"

Delia peeked at her iPhone. "Twenty-two minutes, barring any interruptions along the way."

"We'll scout the area for a good place to position

ourselves, then sit and wait. As far as anyone knows, he's not employed, so his in-and-out of the home pit stops should be more frequent."

"Yeah, makes sense."

"Once we spot Sutton exiting his crib, we'll be on him like a swarm of bees."

"Crib?" Delia repeated, laughing. "Where did you pick up that bit of backstreet vernacular?"

"Should I have said, digs or pad?"

"Maybe you should pick up a copy of Emily Post and read the chapter on the use of proper residential etiquette."

I snorted a chuckle. "You mean for residential criminals?"

Delia continued to laugh.

I pressed down on the accelerator pedal. "Speaking of pit stops, if Sutton is responsible for Holland's disappearance, his next—and his last—pit stop will be the big house."

PART VIII

"Goddamn it," Morelli shouted, banging his fist on the front door of Duggan Investigations. "I should have known Duggan wouldn't stand down and wait like I told him. No doubt he and Delia are out looking for Holland . . . dand it's unlikely either of them knows the Barton girl was reported missing an hour ago."

"Delia's not answering her cell phone?" Agent Anderson asked.

"Hell no. Their phones are either off or in silent mode," Morelli answered in a frustrated tone. "I ought to kick his insubordinate ass smack dab into the middle of the port of Los Angeles."

"And no luck locating any of the gang of three," Anderson continued. "Lundsten's not at the hospital, Shyner's not in his office, and none of the trio were present at their last confirmed home of record per an update by our field agents just twenty minutes ago."

Morelli gave a weary look. "Why do I have the god-awful feeling Duggan's closing in on the whereabouts not only of the gang of three, but Holland, and . . . unknow-ingly, the Barton girl as well? And here we are standing around with our finger up our ass."

Anderson turned and faced Morelli. "Sir, why don't we—"

"Get hold of Blanchard and get her over here. And keep calling Columbo and Nancy Drew," Morelli interrupted, his voice laden with anger.

* * *

"That maniac is going to wind up killing these two," Lundsten confided. Standing next to Melissa and Holland, he directed Shyner's attention to the vials and syringes on the desk. "You've heard me warn Sutton repeatedly that using that drug could be dangerous, especially in their condition."

Shyner threw up his hands. "The problem is he's the one with the gun and the van, and we're stuck here with these two with no way out. We're in this too deep to back out now. Our only alternative is he either kills us, or we somehow contact the authorities and then go to jail for the remainder of our lives, so maybe you should settle down until he returns with whatever he says he has that can counter—"

"Sodium amytal is a barbiturate," Lundsten interrupted. "There are no effective antidotes for the anesthetic they've been administered, which is also a barbiturate. It has to run its course through the patients' own body metabolism."

"Maybe he has something that will—"

Lundsten grabbed a stapler on the desk and flung it against the wall. "You haven't heard a damn thing I've said."

* * *

"Thought you might be interested to know Morelli has tried calling and texting several times," Delia said, toggling between the GPS, Morelli's calls, and text messages.

I took a breath. "He's either called the office, dropped by . . . or both. He'll presume correctly we're out looking for Holland."

"And he won't be happy. Are you going to call him?"

I nodded. "Now that we're in a discreet position outside of Sutton's apartment, we'll make contact with Morelli as soon as we've hooked Sutton and tail him to any place we deem suspicious. If my sixth sense is correct, the big fish will lead us straight to the other fish."

Delia bobbed her head. "It's our only saving grace, considering we were told to stay put. If our fishing expedition confirms there's no Sutton or no fish school in the warehouse, you and I will be sleeping with the fishes . . . or at least the Morelli version of it."

I grumbled, "Don't remind me."

A large white van slowed before making contact with a speed bump next to the non-staffed security booth at the entrance into Sutton's apartment building. Both entry and exit gate arms were fully raised.

"Looks like the apartment complex has some company," I whispered.

"Hmm . . . That seems odd," Delia whispered back, her eyes following the unusually large vehicle resembling a mini-bus. "What is that?"

I stared at the large caravan. "That's a non-emergency medical transport and wheelchair van."

"What makes you so sure?"

"Because I've seen them up close. Check out the raised roof and the elongated sliding door on the right side. Notice the gap in the running board underneath the door; that's where the ramp is located . . . in a small pocket underneath the chassis," I pointed out. "It extends outward and then down at an angle until it rests on the ground—perfect for gurney- and wheelchair-bound patients."

"Okay, so it's a medical and wheelchair transport, which begs the next question: Why would that thing be here at this hour?"

I pressed my lips together and rubbed my chin. "Allow me to answer by asking another question: What does a former Paragon State Hospital employee with a criminal record, a missing concierge with ties to an admitted Paragon psychiatric patient, and a medical transport in our primary suspect's apartment complex at this time in the morning all have in common?"

Delia took in a deep breath. "If we're still tuned in to the same pondering channel, the answer is a former Paragon State Hospital employee and felon by the name of Ray Sutton—who just so happens to reside a few miles from an empty warehouse previously owned by the patient's deceased father."

"I think we're about to find out," I said, peering over the steering wheel for a better look at the medical transport vehicle. Watching the van make a right turn after passing the empty gatehouse and my stealthily concealed sedan, the top-heavy medical transport veered to the left until the driver stopped and double-parked in a row of unoccupied parking spaces outside a ground-level corner apartment. Exiting the van with the parking and side lights illuminated, the operator scurried toward the lighted front door of the unit before fumbling with a key and letting himself inside.

"It's Sutton . . . I'm sure of it," Delia said in a loud whisper. "Did you get a glimpse of his face?"

"I took a quick glance at his criminal history photo. Yep . . . That's our thug." I nodded, squinting for a better look.

Less than two minutes later, the now-identified suspect hopped back inside the van. Switching on the headlights, he drove ahead until the van crossed over and into the next section of sparsely occupied tenant parking spaces. He veered slightly to the right before making a U-turn, then drove back and exited the same way he entered.

"We've hooked our fish," I said. "Let's see where he takes us." Turning the ignition key, I released the parking brake and placed the shift lever in drive.

"He's turning left on East Highland Street." Delia pointed. "Harbor Boulevard is a mile or so east and runs north and south according to the GPS," she murmured, following the blue dot and watching as the screen continuously updated itself in real-time. "He has to turn left on Harbor and drive north another mile and a half to reach the warehouse depot."

"I'm on him," I said.

The van made its way to the far-left turn lane as the vehicle approached and stopped at a red light. I slowed to allow time for the left-turn arrow to illuminate, then continued as I followed the van through the T-intersection and onto Harbor Boulevard, which ran parallel to Los Angeles Harbor.

A mile and a half later, Delia said, "We're approaching the depot."

The van finally turned off Harbor Boulevard and continued for another half-mile down a winding gravelly road leading to a chain-link fence.

"Yeah, I see the warehouses," I said, turning off the headlights and slowing. The van stopped at a chain-link gate. I glanced at Delia. "The entire facility is surrounded by miles of chain-link fencing, topped with barbed wire. It appears that remote gated entry and exit points have been installed in certain sections of the outlying areas; the main entry and exit points more than likely have guardhouses and are staffed around the clock."

"Look." Delia pointed. "The gate is sliding open; Sutton's getting ready to enter the compound."

"It's a card or fob system of some kind that he's privy to," I said. "He's swiping or tapping an active access card or fob to a reader that opens the gate."

"And it will close as soon as he's gone through," Delia replied. "So, what's the plan?"

Watching the van make its way through the opening gate, I uttered a short chuckle, then popped the trunk. "Fetch the bolt cutters."

PART IX

Tossing several packs of Narcan nasal spray on top of the desk in the abandoned office, Sutton stepped back and stared at the small boxes. "These are what I had in my apartment," he revealed. "We'll just spray a canister or two up their noses and let that take effect."

Lundsten shook his head. "You seem to forget that Narcan is used for the treatment of opioid overdoses," he reminded him. "It will not neutralize the effects of the sedative they've been administered. It's useless in this case as an antagonist."

Removing a revolver from his waistband, Sutton raised and pointed the weapon at the disheveled and battered doctor. "Administer the Narcan, Dr. Jekyll, or I'll introduce you to the real Mr. Hyde."

* * *

"Where the hell are you?" Morelli yelled into his cellphone. "I've been calling and texting your evasive ass for more than an hour."

"I've located Sutton. He's—"

"I told you to stay put and wait until—"

I tapped the red disconnect call button on my iPhone.

"He's madder than a grimy skunk dipped in perfume."

"Tell me about it. And dropping the call won't help either. He wasn't even on speaker and I could hear him yelling."

I paused, then took a deep breath. "Let's get through the fence. We'll pursue on foot until we spot the van. Whichever warehouse he's parked next to, that's where he'll be. Then we'll contact Morelli again and wait for the cavalry."

* * *

"From what you've told me, it sounds like Duggan knows where Sutton is, and possibly Melissa Barton and Holland," Blanchard confided in Morelli. "Knowing Duggan like I do, he'll reach out again as soon as he confirms that information."

"So, we're just going to wait for Sherlock Holmes and his assistant, Watson?" Morelli asked sarcastically.

"What can I say?" Blanchard replied in frustration. "Once Matt and Delia have located Sutton, we'll be notified. In the meantime, I suggest we put our SWAT teams on alert. Position your team discreetly outside Sutton's last known address. If Matt gives us a location closer to me than you, my team will be ready to move. Either way, we'll be prepared."

Morelli sighed grudgingly, then turned and looked at his senior agent. "Go ahead and issue the SWAT alert," he ordered, walking past the agent and back toward their unmarked SUV. "Get the team over here as soon as possible."

"I'm on it," Anderson replied.

"I swear I'm going to lock up Duggan as soon as . . ." Morelli's voice trailed off.

* * *

Cutting enough of the chain-link fence to allow entry, I pushed the fence inward before securing it in place with a discarded marker stake. Tossing the bolt cutters aside, I stooped down and crawled through the opening, then helped Delia through. The poorly lit warehouses were strategically built and spaced to facilitate movement and storage of stock and merchandise via an asphalt-covered grid between the buildings.

"It's as quiet as a moth in a cotton box," I whispered, looking in every direction.

"Or the deep blue region of Yellowstone," Delia whispered back.

"These warehouses are either empty, or they're being used to store discarded items and other junk," I muttered. "That would explain why there's no activity in this area."

"Including posted security patrols or vehicle patrols. Perfect for hiding a kidnapped victim," Delia added.

I placed my hand on Delia's arm and we stopped walking. "Del, I'll check out this first row of warehouses on the left. You do the same with the rows on the right." I pointed. "They extend about a hundred yards. Check down the access aisle of each new row of warehouses. Text me if you spot the van. I'll do the same."

"Got it," she acknowledged, scurrying off in the opposite direction.

* * *

Administering a dose of Narcan to Holland and Melissa, the trio waited. After three minutes with no response, a second dose was given. Another three minutes passed, with still no response. Duggan banged his fist against the wall.

"I tried to tell you this wouldn't work," Lundsten grumbled.

Sutton let out a deep breath. "I was prepared for this," he admitted. He began wheeling Holland toward the closed office door.

"Hold on . . . What's plan B?" Shyner asked.

"He doesn't want to wake up, so I'm going to make sure he never does. In the meantime, keep an eye on Sleeping Beauty," he ordered, glancing at Melissa. "She's an escapee and will be sent back to the hospital for permanent admission."

"He's going to kill that man," Lundsten whispered to Shyner.

* * *

Del, I've spotted the van, I texted.

Where are you? she replied.

Eight rows down and to the right; the fifth warehouse on the left. Contact Morelli and let him know our location, then head back to the gate and wait for him to arrive.

Will do.

The medical transport van was parked unoccupied next to a mini-warehouse. A small aluminum service entry door on the side of the building opposite the van was part of the framework. I grabbed the doorknob and turned it, but it was locked. I took out a credit card-size lock pick set from my jacket pocket. Stooping down, I inserted a pick and tension wrench into the keyway, probing and twisting until the plug and knob turned with the wrench. I turned the round handle all the way to the left, then carefully entered before closing the door behind me.

Hearing a noise, I drew my holstered revolver and quickly moved behind a dusty metal shelf a few feet to the left of the door. A silhouette of a wheelchair being pushed by a large figure emerged, visible from the office door about twenty-five feet straight ahead. Squinting, I tried to make out the two figures bathed in the soft glow of the fluorescent light.

Sufferin' cats—that's Sutton . . . and Holland in the chair.

PART X

Pushing the wheelchair-bound concierge out of the warehouse side door and toward the medical transport vehicle, Sutton stopped and reached down, locking the wheels in preparation for loading the occupied chair back inside the van. "All right, Mr. Stumbling Block," he mumbled in a mocking voice, "you've been an annoying obstacle and thorn in my side long enough. If it weren't for you, my elitist snob of a cousin would be enjoying permanent residency in the nuthouse, and I would be enjoying the Barton inheritance. Now it's time to cash in your chips and get tossed out of the casino . . . for good. All that remains is to—"

"Hold it right there," I yelled out, stepping out of the warehouse and aiming my revolver at Sutton's upper torso.

Startled, the unscrupulous felon looked around, expecting to see other uniformed officers. Regaining his composure, he turned and faced me, a malevolent grin appearing. "Okay, I give up . . . Who the hell are you?"

"Never mind who I am," I retorted, noticing the gun behind Sutton's belt. "Use your left hand and take that pistol out of your waistband . . . nice and slow . . . and throw it over the top of the van. Get stupid, and I'll put a hollow point right between your eyes."

Sutton gave a cynical chuckle. "So, you're a private

dick," he correctly surmised. "Well, this is all very clever of you," he said as he tossed the gun over the van. "Was it Holland who hired you?"

I snickered. "Yeah, as a matter of fact, it was, and it's all on video," I said, motioning in the direction of my iPhone propped up on top of a broom and rake organizer mounted on the side of the warehouse. "I've got enough on you right now to guarantee you won't be anyone's problem again for at least twenty years." I gazed at Holland. "If anything happens to that man, the last thing you'll ever see is a needle being stuck in your arm."

Sutton pretended to sigh in resignation before pausing. "Well, it looks like you've got me, gumshoe. I suppose I'd better—" He pushed Holland's wheelchair onto its side then sprinted around the back of the van, racing toward the discarded weapon.

I charged around the front of the vehicle and tackled the co-conspirator. The impact knocked my gun out of my hand. Sutton struggled to break free and reach the revolver, which was now within arm's reach. Holding firm and rising to my feet, I tried to pull the convicted felon up from the ground. A kick to my chest sent me sprawling onto my back. The desperate suspect turned over and crawled furiously toward his gun. He reached the pistol and sat upright, swinging his arm around in an attempt to point the weapon at its intended target.

The sound of gunfire echoed throughout the maze of warehouses and empty pathways between the buildings.

Sutton stared at me with a blank expression before slowly tumbling onto his side. His pistol bounced off the dark asphalt.

Holding tight to my .38-caliber backup revolver, which I had just pulled out of my ankle holster, I stood up and walked toward the motionless Sutton. There was no movement, and it appeared that he was not breathing. I kicked his gun a safe distance away and retrieved my dropped pistol. Then, I stooped down and placed my index and middle finger on Sutton's carotid artery. There was no pulse.

I hurried around the van and helped Holland, who was unsteady on his feet, stand up. The fall from the wheelchair had shaken him out of his sedated state.

"Are you okay?" I asked.

Holland shook his head, trying to clear his mind. "Wha . . . what the hell is going on? Where am I?" he asked in a trembling voice.

"You're safe now," I reassured him. "It appears Sutton and his two cohorts abducted you, which is why you're in front of this warehouse. Based on what I could see and hear, he was preparing you for a one-way swim in the ocean."

Unfazed by the realization that he was only a short journey away from a permanent rendezvous with Davy Jones's locker, Holland looked around anxiously. "Hold on. If I'm here . . . where's Melissa?"

I looked at him with confusion. "Melissa? What do you—"

"Wait a minute . . . what's that?" Holland interrupted, pointing.

I followed his gaze and squinted my eyes. I could see a caravan of tactical and police vehicles approaching down the service aisle, about ten warehouses away. "Looks like the Mounties have arrived," I blurted out. Law enforcement personnel in tactical gear emerged from the vehicles, forming a semi-circle on the opposite side of the medical transport. Two fire rescue trucks and ambulances remained at a discreet distance. Delia, Morelli, and Blanchard jumped out of an unmarked SUV and cautiously approached

Holland and me, crouching with their weapons drawn.

"Are you two okay?" Delia asked in a hushed tone.

"We're good," I told her. Holland confirmed with a thumbs up.

Morelli gave me the stink eye again. "We'll talk more later."

"Where's Melissa . . . and where are Lundsten and Shyner?" Blanchard chimed in.

I glanced at Delia, a puzzled look on my face. "Melissa?"

"Morelli informed me on the way here that she was reported missing shortly after Holland disappeared."

I wheeled around and surveyed the warehouse, pondering Delia's statement. "Then there's a very high probability she's in that same office inside the building."

A commotion emerging from the warehouse utility door caught everyone's attention. "Don't shoot, don't shoot!"

The tactical team turned and faced the door, their weapons aimed at its rectangular center. His hands raised high in the air, a slovenly Shyner waddled awkwardly through the opening and onto the asphalt aisleway, his eyes filled with terror.

"Everyone, hold your fire," Blanchard yelled out.

"Stop!" Morelli shouted using a bullhorn. "Turn around; place your hands on your head and interlace your fingers," he ordered, pointing his Sig Sauer semi-auto pistol at the rotund lawyer. Several SWAT officers took aim with their assault rifles.

The terrified attorney complied, completing an about-face and placing his clasped hands on top of his head.

"Slowly . . . Begin walking back toward the sound of my voice," Morelli shouted, Shyner again complying with the order. Two SWAT officers crept cautiously toward the portly esquire, grabbing and half-dragging him hurriedly back and around Blanchard's unmarked SUV.

Blanchard snatched Shyner and spun him around. "Where's Melissa . . . and where is Lundsten?"

"They're holed up inside the warehouse," he sputtered.

"Where in the warehouse?" Morelli jumped in.

"In an abandoned office in the center of the building," Shyner said. "She's sedated and safely restrained in a wheel-chair. Lundsten's in there with her."

"You'd better be right," Morelli said sternly. He ordered Shyner to sit on the ground next to the unmarked SUV before cuffing and securing him to the running board. He turned and placed his hand on Agent Anderson's shoulder. "You just heard him. Out of an abundance of caution, we'll need to treat this as a hostage situation. Choose three team members and prepare for a deliberate entry into that facility. The goal is to locate and neutralize Lundsten in unison with the safe release and retrieval of Melissa. You know the drill. Advise when ready."

"Got it. Let's go," Anderson yelled out, calling aside three officers for a quick briefing.

* * *

"You're a stain on the profession," the masked and dark-clothed figure ranted in a muffled tone, walking in a menacing gait toward Lundsten as he backed away from the unidentified party. Holding a large pair of metal shearing scissors, the concealed figure continued to approach the bedraggled physician.

"Who are you? What do you want?" the panicked psychiatrist implored.

Ignoring the question, the shadowy figure continued

to advance. "You're everything a mental health professional should not be," came the reply. "You're a loathsome scoundrel and a cad. You and your two cohorts have caused irreparable harm to countless patients, and in so doing have further stained the reputation of Paragon State Hospital. Not to mention, you're guilty of the worst kind of despicable fraud by conspiring to have an innocent young woman deemed mentally incompetent."

"It was all Sutton's doing," Lundsten said, glancing back and forth between the perp's covered face and his long-bladed shears. "It was all his idea," he repeated. "He was the mastermind," he yelled out, continuing to back away.

"And all for the purpose of having her committed for the remainder of her life . . . or at least long enough so you and your criminal co-conspirators could plunder the ill-gotten gains of her deceased father's shipping empire," the unidentified perpetrator sneered.

"I . . . I was in the process of turning this whole thing around," Lundsten stammered, continuing to back away. "I, I . . . I was going to turn in Sutton and Shyner." He looked around, his fear and anxiety intensifying. "If it weren't for me, Melissa wouldn't even be alive," he said, his tone of voice growing desperate. "I tried to protect her. You . . . you've got to believe me."

The disguised figure ignored Lundsten's lame attempts to rationalize his unprofessional and criminal behavior. "If it weren't for you and your evil cohorts, none of this would have happened. You could have cost this innocent young woman and her concierge their lives. And for that, there is no forgiveness."

Knowing his time was up, the disgraced doctor turned and bolted in a desperate attempt to reach the warehouse-side utility door.

The covered culprit scurried after Lundsten, catching up with him and plunging the shearing scissors deep into the middle of his back. The discredited psychiatrist fell forward, a sickening crack reverberating throughout the warehouse as his forehead made contact with the smooth concrete floor. The perpetrator stared for a moment at the motionless doctor, then disappeared into the darkness.

* * *

"The warehouse is secure," Anderson reported to Morelli ten minutes later, speaking into his radio. "Melissa Barton has been located inside the abandoned office. She's unconscious but otherwise appears unharmed."

"And Lundsten?"

"We found him face down in a pool of blood, halfway between the office and the service entry-side door, a pair of metal shears protruding out of the middle of his back . . . all the way to the grip handles. He's dead."

Blanchard gave the go-ahead for the medics and fire rescue to enter the warehouse and attend to Melissa, then turned and looked at Shyner. "Someone take this sorry excuse for a lawyer and place him in the back seat of a patrol vehicle."

"I'll do it," I offered in a disgusted tone, walking toward Shyner, still cuffed to the SUV's running board.

"I'll go with you," Delia said, escorting Shyner to an MPD patrol car obscured by a larger SWAT vehicle.

"Aren't you going to re-cuff me?" Shyner asked, glancing back and forth between Delia and me as we approached the police cruiser.

Delia grinned snidely. "Why? Planning to escape?"

"You'd like that, wouldn't you? Oh, and by the way, I

know all about you, lady."

Reaching the patrol vehicle, I handed the cuffs to Delia. "Turn around and lean against the vehicle, smart-ass. Put your hands behind your back."

"It's all the same to me," Shyner arrogantly replied. "I'm an attorney. I know the system and I know how to manipulate it. I'll be out of lockup and back in my office before you two return to your own. That's what I'll do, and that's what I have to say."

Delia took a step back. "Oh, really? You say? Well, before that happens, there is something I'd like to say."

Shyner responded with a slow smirk. "Not that I give a shit, Ms. Detective-Widow-turned-Private-Investigator and gumshoe bitch, but what would that be?" he asked in a hateful tone.

"This," Delia thundered, delivering a roundhouse kick, her boot connecting with the left side of Shyner's bloated face. He dropped to the ground like a sack of potatoes. Standing over the unconscious attorney, she shouted, "That's for Melissa and Holland, and for all the other innocent patients and clients you've lied to, cheated, and ruined . . . You rotten, bottom-feeding, ambulance-chasing pettifogger."

"Daaaamn," I howled out loud, a smile flashing over my face. "You're right, Del . . . he was trying to escape."

PART XI

"Whoa, Morelli's really giving it to him this time," Delia announced, standing in the hallway outside the FBI conference room. She could hear the bureau's lead agent tearing into Matt through the closed doors.

"I hope he's wearing a set of ass plates," Holland added.

"Wearing what?" Agent Anderson asked, appearing puzzled.

"He's being facetious," Delia replied.

"Morelli's making Gunny's rant of chew-outs from the movie *Full Metal Jacket* look like a pleasant sermon," Agent Anderson chimed in. "The last thing you ever want is to be on the receiving end of an ass-chewing from that guy. And I can tell you that from personal experience, trust me."

"It doesn't help that everyone's been up all night," Delia said. She glanced at her watch. It was a little after eight in the morning. Looking up, she noticed attorney Erin Lauber turning the corner down the hallway, headed in their direction. Delia tapped Holland's arm, then motioned in Lauber's direction.

"Hey there," Holland piped up.

"Hi everyone," Lauber cheerfully announced. She was modestly dressed in a blue pantsuit covered by a tan all-weather coat. Enfolding Holland in a warm embrace, she then turned and gave Delia a quick hug.

"So, what's the word?" Delia asked.

"It's good." Lauber grinned. "But before I say anything, who is this handsome, dark-suited gentleman?" she asked, craning her head at the male standing next to Holland.

"Oops," Delia blurted. "I guess I'm more fatigued than I thought." She pivoted around and placed her hand on Anderson's arm. "This is Assistant Lead Agent John Anderson. He's part of the FBI investigation team assigned to this case."

Lauber smiled, then extended her hand. "Nice to meet you, Agent Anderson."

"My pleasure," he said, shaking her hand in return.

"All right," Lauber began. "I just left the hospital where Melissa has been admitted. Everett contacted me subsequent to Delia and Matt's successful investigation, followed by the FBI and MPD joint operation. She's scheduled for a complete physical and psychological exam this afternoon. She's in a private room and resting comfortably."

"Speaking of our joint operation," Agent Anderson chimed in, "what's the situation regarding the remaining Paragon patients who were wrongfully admitted?"

"A court order will be issued shortly and delivered to Paragon ordering their release and transport to the same hospital for evaluation," Erin explained. "I met the presiding judge in his chambers early this morning. Afterward, they will be free to return home to their families."

"I smell the aroma of numerous lawsuits stirring in the air," Holland proclaimed.

"More like an odor," Delia groused.

"That's a whole other issue," Lauber responded. She turned and faced Holland again. "I heard you declined the offer to be checked out at the same hospital."

"I'm okay. It's Melissa we're all concerned about."

"Trust me, she's going to be just fine," Lauber reassured Holland, placing her hand on his shoulder. She craned her head in the direction of the conference room. "What's all that yelling I'm hearing?" she asked.

"That's Matt getting an earful from Morelli," Delia replied.

Lauber shook her head and sighed. "Let me guess. Because he didn't stand down like he was told until permission was received from J. Edgar Hoover in there, he's catching hell . . . am I right?"

Everyone gave a slight nod.

"Yeah, well, it's time to yank that plug out of the wall," she declared in a heavy voice. As she walked toward the conference room double doors, Agent Anderson sprinted ahead and attempted to block her."

"Ma'am, please don't go in there," he pleaded. "I'm sure whatever is going on, it'll be over soon."

"It's over right now," Lauber retorted. "Move out of my way, Agent Anderson."

Anderson paused, letting out a heavy breath before reluctantly stepping aside.

She grabbed the door handle and yanked it open, barreling through like a Chicago Bears linebacker.

* * *

Morelli and I stood at the far end of the conference room table. Caught off guard, we both turned our heads, surprised.

"Who gave you permission to barge in?" Morelli snarled.

Lauber scurried up to the lead FBI agent. "This interrogation is over."

"It's not an interrogation," Morelli angrily fired back.

I smirked. "It's an ass-chewing, for not—"

"I don't care what it's for," Lauber interrupted. She exchanged glances with both of us, then locked eyes with Morelli. "If it weren't for this man," she said, turning and glancing at me, "both Melissa and Everett might be dead, not to mention the danger Delia was willing to risk by pretending to be suicidal in order to be admitted inside that looney bin." She paused. "If you have a problem with what I'm telling you, then go and get Grissinger and bring him in here, otherwise . . . you're done."

Morelli's face took on a furious look. Without saying another word, he picked up a manila file lying on the table and exited the conference room, slamming the door behind him.

I looked at Erin and snorted a chuckle. "He wanted to lambast Delia as well. I told him he'd have to kick my ass before I'd allow that to happen."

Lauber smiled. "You're an excellent investigator, Matt. That could have something to do with Morelli's fury."

I furrowed my brow. "You mean professional jealousy?"

Erin placed her arms around my neck. "It was you who located Melissa and Holland, not Morelli. Seems like you're always one step ahead. It doesn't make him look good when a retired police detective turned private investigator does a better job than his distinguished FBI colleague."

"Morelli's my friend. It's not a competition."

"Nevertheless, I want to thank you for what you did on behalf of my client, Melissa, and my dear friend, Everett." Standing on her toes, she leaned in to kiss me, her perky breasts poking the front of my chest like darts on a game board, my hands resting on her hips as I drew her in.

Easing out of our embrace, I locked eyes with my client's attorney. "You might not want to thank me too quickly," I murmured with a half-smile.

Reacting with a puzzled look, she asked, "What do you mean?"

Reaching into my dress shirt pocket, I removed a small card. "This, to start," I said, revealing a standard-size foil calling card containing her law firm's details.

Erin gave the card a hard look. "Yes, it's my business card. What's that got to do with anything?"

"It fell out of Shyner's shirt pocket after his arrest . . . before he was transported to the local jail."

Lauber shook her head. "I don't get it. What was he doing with it?"

Walking around the conference table and holding the card by its edge, I stopped abruptly and turned around. "Shyner claims he picked it up off the floor of the warehouse, right before he walked out of the facility with his hands held high in the air. He said the gold foil on the card gleamed, even in the darkened building."

Erin shrugged. "So what? I wouldn't trust anything that two-bit lying huckster says. He's finished as an attorney. Even if he pleads guilty, he'll die in prison." She paused, then gave an anxious look. "Do you believe him?"

"That he picked up the card in the warehouse? Yes, as a matter of fact, I do, but not because he was interested in any legal advice from you." I continued, "But it does beg the question: Why was your card in that warehouse at that specific time?"

Lauber pulled a face. "Everett must have been carrying it with him," she speculated. "We've known each other for years. He's taken several of my cards. Maybe it was in his pocket when Sutton abducted and wheeled him into the—"

"Wearing a hospital gown?" I cut in. "Hospital gowns don't have pockets."

Erin looked at me for a long while, this time without expression. "Just what are you getting at?" she finally asked.

"And were you aware that the previous hospital administrator, Milton O'Toole, was reported missing from Paragon during the early morning hours encompassing the abduction of Melissa and Holland?" I continued, ignoring her question.

"I have no idea what you're talking about."

"And I'm sure you'll tell me you don't know anything about why your business cards were found in O'Toole's dark-colored clothing scattered about his room, and among his personal effects after he mysteriously returned to Paragon later that same morning?"

"I'm not saying another thing," she abruptly fired back.

"Good job, Matt," a voice in the background said.

Erin spun around. FBI attorney Grissinger and lead FBI Agent Morelli were standing several feet away, having walked into the room through a concealed door in the wall behind the opposite end of the oval conference table.

"We have O'Toole in another room," Morelli announced. "Unlike Ms. Lauber here, he's singing like a canary, to quote the infamous phrase. It's all on video."

"Enough that we can arrest and charge both of you with criminal conspiracy and the murder of Doctor Lundsten," Grissinger added. He turned and looked at Morelli.

"Read Judge Judy her rights."

PART XII

"So, what do you think of this detective theater restaurant?" I asked, pulling Delia's chair away from our assigned table, then gently pushing it back as she sat.

She flashed an edgy smile; her demeanor appeared cool and indifferent. She picked up a glass of water and took a sip. "The interrogation reception was interesting," she said, her tone chilly. Checking out a menu placed next to her dinnerware, she quickly glanced over the three entrees listed before tossing the menu back onto the table.

"I think it'll be fun," I ventured, noticing Delia's lack of interest. "I'm told these murder-mystery dinner shows base their scripts on present-day, loosely based actual FBI cold cases. The actors not only stay in character throughout the evening, but a few are seated at the tables and are revealed as the investigation progresses throughout the show. Some guests even become prime suspects. I hear it's very hands-on . . . keeps everyone on their toes," I said, smiling and looking around. "I've even heard . . ."

"Hold on a second," Delia interrupted, raising her eyes and staring at me. "All I want to know is . . . who killed Dr. Lundsten?"

An awkward pause followed. "That's now the problem of the FBI and MPD."

A look of frustration crept over Delia's face. "As usual, I can't get a straight answer to a straight question." Hesitating, she turned again and locked eyes with me. "I know you know who did it," she objected.

"I've already gone over this with you, Del," I replied in an exasperated tone.

"Go over it again," she insisted.

I looked up, then took a deep breath. "Both O'Toole and Lauber had motives. According to Shyner, on the night of O'Toole's psychotic episode, it was Lundsten who had earlier spiked O'Toole's coffee with an overdose of ketamine. It wasn't surprising when he was subsequently Baker Acted and taken to Paragon after the incident at the car dealership, where a court later extended his involuntary admission. Not only did he lose his job as chief medical superintendent, but then, to add insult to injury, he was succeeded by Lundsten. That's your motive for O'Toole."

"And Lauber?"

"Lauber hated Shyner because he was a greedy, low-life ambulance-chasing attorney scoundrel and was part of the same conspiratorial plot to court sanction the permanent confinement of her client, Melissa Barton, to Paragon. As additional insurance, the scheme to eliminate loyal family concierge Everett Holland, who was a very good friend of Lauber, would make it easier for the gang of three to successfully pursue their plan of divvying up Barton Shipping and pillaging its assets . . . or at least they thought so."

Delia looked perplexed. "What I don't understand is—"

"Lundsten and Shyner were both targeted for murder," I broke in, "except there wasn't enough time, and Lundsten just happened to venture outside that makeshift office inside the warehouse only moments before the SWAT teams arrived. There was only enough time to kill one. The murderer must have already known Sutton was dead, although he—or she—wanted to make it a trifecta . . . or at least that was the original intent."

"What was the connection between O'Toole and Lauber?"

"You mean based on Lauber's calling cards that were found in O'Toole's possession?"

"That and O'Toole's interrogation by the FBI."

"Someone reached out to the other," I reasoned. "Either O'Toole contacted Lauber subsequent to his railroading, or Lauber contacted O'Toole out of a sense of duty and empathy, and the fact her client and Holland were victims of the same perpetrating trio."

Delia pursed her lips in frustration. "So . . . who is it?"

"Hey, we did our job," I reminded her. "We located Melissa and Holland, and then led the authorities to the exact location . . . and before either were physically harmed." I reached over and touched Delia's arm, then gave an affectionate smile. "As far as I'm concerned, the *best* thing that happened was not having to follow through on your idea of faking a mental health crisis for the purpose of admission into that hellhole."

"You're about to cause me a *real* mental health crisis," Delia protested.

"You have no idea how worried I was," I confessed. "You've got more moxie than most men I know," I told her.

A sudden gleam appeared in her eyes. "You really mean that?" she asked, a half-smile appearing.

"I really do," I said, returning a confirming gaze.

Delia beamed her approval. "Okay, so who—"

"It's Morelli and Blanchard's responsibility now,"

I repeated, leaning back in my chair. "It's also their responsibility to unravel all the particulars regarding the conspiracy to commit Melissa and plunder Barton Shipping. The good news is I'm confident Melissa will be up and running her late father's shipping empire in short order, with a very good friend and fatherly figure guiding and advising her."

Delia fidgeted, a grumpy look returning and replacing her previous cheerful demeanor. "You're playing with me, and you're doing it deliberately. So, you're not going to tell me who Lundsten's murderer is . . . are you?"

Hesitating for a moment, I looked around the dinner theater. "Aren't you curious as to why theatre management allowed us inside just before opening . . . and before seating the other paying customers for tonight's show?"

"I assumed it was your way of arranging for the best table," Delia said in a sulky tone.

I shook my head. "I contacted theater management several days ago while you were at lunch. As part of making reservations, I told them who I was, and asked, as part of tonight's murder mystery, if they'd be open to setting a scene for a murder mystery based on a scenario known only to you and me, and which will occur during our evening here . . . And to my pleasant surprise, they agreed. Remember, guests are encouraged to interact with each other and the characters to solve the mystery."

Delia returned a baffled look. "Okay, so what does all of this have to do with the identity of Lundsten's murderer?"

I returned a playful smile. "Everything," I said. "If you successfully solve tonight's murder mystery, you'll know exactly who the murderer is, but without anyone else knowing. We'll both participate and play along, but it's up to you to figure it out."

Delia let out a deep breath. "I can't believe you're doing this."

"Doing what?"

"Making me participate in this playhouse theatre version of Clue to figure out what you already know. We may as well go back to the office and break out the board game. Professor Plum did it in the conservatory with a gun," she mockingly replied.

I chuckled. "Except in our case, it was a pair of metal shearing scissors," I gently reminded her. "And I might add it's always been you who suggested we dine or go out for coffee after wrapping up a successful investigation, but this time I beat you to it. I thought this would be fun, and ultimately revealing regarding your question." Pausing, I reached over and gently squeezed her hand. "However, if you'd rather not do this, we can leave, but you're going to miss a great dinner and a great show. Just say the word and we'll go."

Delia exhaled a sigh of resignation, then cracked a cheeky grin. "And not know the murderer's identity before the FBI and MPD figure it out?" She leaned forward and gazed at me. "You know, maybe this will be fun after all."

"Yeah, it will," I said, with a happy expression. I turned and pointed. "Look, management is now allowing guests to enter the restaurant. The ushers are escorting everyone to their assigned tables." I checked my watch. "The dinner and show will begin soon."

Scooting her chair closer, she placed her hand on my arm. "Before dinner and the show begin, can I tell you something?"

"Sure . . . fire away."

"Your friend Morelli is definitely right about one thing."

I returned a curious look. "And what would that be?"

"You're a ball buster."

Snorting in amusement, I said, "So I've been told."

We gazed at each other for a long moment, the chummy stare-down ending with a simultaneous outburst of laughter.

THE END

www.ingramcontent.com/pod-product-compliance
Lightning Source LLC
Chambersburg PA
CBHW062204270326
41930CB00009B/1639